Visitor
Au
TYROL & V

C000162258

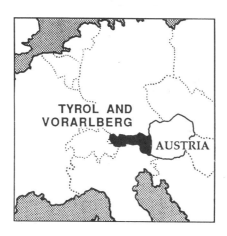

TYROL AND
VORARLBERG

AUSTRIA

# VISITOR'S GUIDE
# AUSTRIA:
# TYROL
## and
# VORARLBERG

## ALAN PROCTOR

MPC

HUNTER
PUBLISHING INC

Published by:
Moorland Publishing Co Ltd,
Moor Farm Road West,
Ashbourne,
Derbyshire DE6 1HD
England

ISBN 0 86190 433 8

Published in the USA by:
Hunter Publishing Inc,
300 Raritan Center Parkway,
CN 94, Edison, NJ 08818
ISBN 1 55650 473 X (USA)

British Library Cataloguing in
Publication Data:
A catalogue record for this book is
available from the British Library.

Colour origination by:
P. & W. Graphics Pte Ltd, Singapore

Printed in the UK by:
Richard Clay Ltd, Bungay, Suffolk

Cover photograph: *The village of
Going and the Wilder Kaiser
mountains* (Tony Stone Associates
Ltd).

Illustrations have been supplied as
follows: A. Proctor: p11, 63, 66, 67,
85, 86, 107 top, 122, 155 bottom;
Ron Scholes: 15, 18 bottom, 54, 91
top, 94 bottom, 111, 114, 115, 118;
all other illustrations are from the
MPC Picture Collection.

MPC Production Team:
*Editorial*: Tonya Monk
*Design*: Jonathan Moss and John
  Robey
*Cartography*: Alastair Morrison
*Typesetting*: Christine Haines

# CONTENTS

## Key to Symbols Used in Text Margin and on Maps

| | | | |
|---|---|---|---|
| 亽 | Recommended walk | ♦ | Church/Monastery |
| 🐾 | Nature reserve/Animal interest | 🏛 | Building of interest |
| ❀ | Garden | 🏰 | Castle/Fortification |
| 🚂 | Steam Railway | 🖼 | Museum/Art gallery |
| 🎾 | Sports facilities | 🌲 | Beautiful view/Scenery, Natural phenomenon |
| ✳ | Other place of interest | 🎿 | Skiing facilities |
| | | ⛵ | Boating facilities |

## Key to Maps

| | | | |
|---|---|---|---|
| ▬▬▬ | Main road | ▦ | ● City/Town |
| ═══ | Autobahn (Motorway) | ～⌒～ | River/Lake |

### How To Use This Guide

This MPC Visitor's Guide has been designed to be as easy to use as possible. Each chapter covers a region or itinerary in a natural progression which gives all the background information to help you enjoy your visit. MPC's distinctive margin symbols, the important places printed in bold, and a comprehensive index enable the reader to find the most interesting places to visit with ease. At the end of each chapter an Additional Information section gives specific details such as addresses and opening times, making this guide a complete sightseeing companion. At the back of the guide the Fact File, arranged in alphabetical order, gives practical information and useful tips to help you plan your holiday — before you go and while you are there. The maps of each region show the main towns, villages, roads and places of interest, but are not designed as route maps and motorists should always use a good recommended road atlas.

## THE AUTHOR

Alan Proctor has been a frequent visitor to Austria for the past 30 years and has been walking there since 1976. He is the author or co-author, of eleven books on walking and travel, both in Austria and in Great Britain, including *Off the Beaten Track: Austria* and *The Visitor's Guide to Somerset, Dorset and Wiltshire*, both published by MPC. Since 1979 he has led parties of walkers in the Tyrol for a national holiday company.

He lives in Wiltshire where he runs a business in leisure activities, escorting small groups in the pursuit of walking, canoeing and mountain biking. He is married to the novelist, Patricia Lawson.

## ACKNOWLEDGEMENTS

The author and publisher would like to offer their grateful thanks to the Austrian Tourist Board, London, and to Lindsey Porter for providing extra material and information on the Vorarlberg.

In memory of Mattie who first introduced me to Austria;
and whose heart always remained there.

# PREFACE

Austria probably has more variety to offer than any other European country. The towns seem to have a timeless air about them, while villages step out from picture postcards.

Travelling about the country brings one face to face with a culture developed over centuries. Many imposing castles, survivors of the Middle Ages, dominate the valleys and these have often been converted into comfortable hotels or restaurants.

The welcome is always kind, smiling and sincere and tourists are never made to feel that they are intruders. Folklore is especially strong and in the evenings many hotels or restaurants have a folk event, which may simply be two or three people with zither and guitar, but almost always there are songs in which the visitor is invited to join.

The abbeys and parish churches, mostly Baroque, are exquisite examples of religious art. Above, tower the mountains, many of which carry snow all year round. Two thirds of Austria is mountainous: in summer it is a paradise for walkers, in winter a paradise for skiers. Most of the ski lifts operate all year round, so that the summer walker can be swiftly transported to the heights.

# INTRODUCTION

T he youngest, and possibly the most thriving, industry in Austria is tourism. The genuine friendliness of the people is evident for all to see. One may meet the zither player from last night's entertainment going about his everyday job; he will take time to greet people, shake hands and wish them a happy holiday, all with a beaming smile.

Music is of prime importance and, though the tourist may not be able to visit the opera, every village has its quota of entertainments, ranging from a single quiet zither player, to a group of yodellers, or a full scale Tyrolean dance troupe. A Tyrolean evening with a shoe platter group is a delight and the visitor may well be drawn into the dancing.

Village festivals occur at frequent intervals, are a photographer's paradise and a great favourite with tourists. Yet they are part of the everyday life of the village, not a display. The clergy, village dignitaries, firemen and rifle brigade, all dressed in traditional costume, are followed by the villagers, all proudly maintaining centuries of tradition.

Food and drink are taken seriously in Austria. With such a rich historical past they have adopted and Austrianised dishes from other countries. The visitor can experiment the menu without fear. No fiery concoctions will attack the palate or stomach. However, it may be advisable to watch the waistline: Austrians eat well and often, while portions tend to be large and filling.

Restaurants, coffee shops, and the ubiquitous guest houses all have one thing in common — their excellent service. There is never any hurry. One sits and waits for the waiter who, with a

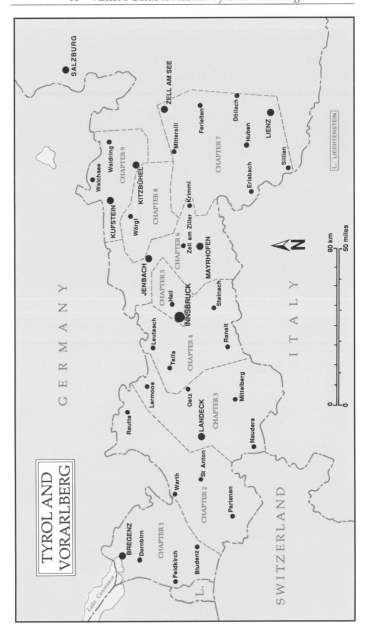

*A roadside fountain made from local materials*

gracious *bitte sehr*, will take one's order. The problem may be in paying, as there is never any suggestion that one should drink up and go. A single coffee or glass of beer can last all evening if one desires. Trying to catch the waiter's eye to pay can take time, but a gentle *Zahlen Bitte* (pay please) as he goes by is the best way.

One of the most civilised things is for families to take a break, the children with an ice cream, the adults with either coffee or a glass of beer, at any time of day. The Austrians have a word for it — *gemutlichkeit* —for the happy jovial atmosphere.

To describe a town or village as picturesque is to declare it as outstanding. Almost all are decorative and most houses have window boxes and balconies filled with flowers, while many have delightful mural paintings.

## History

From the earliest times Austria has been a pageant of people on the move. The Romans conquered it and, amazingly, kept a road open through the Alps all year round — quite a feat even today at the higher levels. Armies, traders, and settlers came and went — Goths, the Vandals, Attila the Hun, Teutons, Slavs, Franks and Burgundians. They were followed by the Magyars of Hungary who devasted the country until they were defeated by the Franks and Bavarians. In AD800 Charlemagne was crowned emperor by the Pope but his mighty empire was divided after his death.

At the end of the thirteenth-century the House of Habsburg came to rule over Austria, a rule which was to continue until 1918. During this time they survived the plots, intrigues and wars which raged round Europe and their empire. Most important, perhaps, was the 200-year struggle against the Turks waged during the sixteenth and seventeenth centuries, culminating in a massive Turkish defeat and the preservation of a Christian Europe. In this period Austria became the centre of the Counter-Reformation.

Early in the eighteenth century one of the greatest queens in history came to the throne. Maria Theresa was a great reformer. She gathered the feudal states together under a central adminis-tration and reformed trade, education, and the church. Her reign was a golden era for cultural expansion, the age of Haydn and Mozart, and high Baroque in art and architecture.

Napoleon transformed Europe. Among other things, he defeated the German princes and humiliated them by placing them under his own authority. He subsequently married an Austrian princess in an attempt to stabilise his position in Europe.

The next figure to arise was Bismarck, who wished to unite Germany under one rule, dominated by Prussia but excluding Austria. In 1866, along with his new ally Italy, he attacked Austria. The Austrians defeated the Italians but were in turn beaten by Bismarck at Sadowa in Bohemia.

World War I brought disaster and disintegration to the Habsburg Empire. At the end of the war the German-speaking areas were formed into the Republic of Austria, while the Magyars, Poles, Croats, Czechs, Slovaks, and other unwilling subjects of the Habsburgs, created new countries for themselves. This period of Austria's history was a disaster. What had been built up as a great empire, with lines of communication centred on Vienna, was now only a tiny remnant. Produce was cut off from its markets, and ports from their hinterland. Financial chaos and hyper-inflation raged.

Chancellor Dollfuss took office in 1932. Dollfuss feared the Nazis who had proclaimed plans to incorporate Austria into Germany, and in 1934, after Parliament was dissolved, they tried to bring about a civil war. It lasted for 5 days, after which Dollfuss turned his one-party rule into a dictatorship. He was later murdered and his successor, Schuschnigg, could not resist the pressure. In March 1938 German troops marched unopposed into Austria and eighteen months later World War II began.

In May 1945 Austria was occupied by the Russians, then by the French, American and British forces. Though many troops had retired earlier, a peace treaty was not signed until May 1955.

Modern Austria is a Democratic Federal Republic divided into nine federal states. She holds a respected position in international affairs, lending active support to the work of the United Nations, but is not currently a member of the European Economic Community (EEC).

## The Vorarlberg

The Vorarlberg lies between Lake Constance, Switzerland, Germany, and the Arlberg mountains. Here, from the eastern shores of the lake, green fields give way to gentle tree covered hills, which in turn rise up to the mighty mountains of the Arlberg. The motorway and main road speeds through-traffic from Bregenz, via the Arlberg Tunnel, into the Tyrol. In doing so, they miss much which is worth seeing. The wise traveller will take the side roads to fully appreciate this beautiful area.

It has something to offer everyone, from a steamer trip on Lake Constance to a walk in high mountain country at about 2,000m (6,560ft). The forest of the Bregenzerwald covers much of the northern part of the region. There are delights such as the Walsertal, a peaceful valley which has no through road. The Hochtannberg Pass would make an exciting day tour, with picturesque villages to explore on the way. High mountains round Damuls attract climbers from a wide area, while to the south are more peaceful valleys reaching up to the great mountains on the border with Liechtenstein and Switzerland.

Another exciting day's tour is that of the Montafon valley. Here, at the end of the valley close to the village of Partenen, the Silvretta High Alpine Road begins. It opens up a spectacular alpine region and can also be used as a route into the Tyrol.

# The Tyrol

Over the Arlberg Pass, now an all-weather road, there is a long descent into the Tyrol. The mighty River Inn is reached at Landeck and runs along the valley to Kufstein, where it enters Germany. The Inn rises in Switzerland to the south of the Silvretta range and crosses the border into Austria near Nauders. Between Nauders and Ried is the Oberinntal where the tourist authority claims it to be a scientific fact that the sun shines longer and more brightly than anywhere else.

This long valley runs easterly, then north-easterly nearer Kufstein. Also running north-easterly from the Arlberg is the famous Lechtal. Both the River Lech and the River Inn run into the Danube, which eventually flows into the Black Sea.

Reaching out from the main Inn valley are side valleys, some with dead ends as far as the motorist is concerned, others like the Wipp Tal carrying main routes. The Wipp Tal leads to the Brenner Pass, now crossed by a motorway.

Eastward the next major valleys lie just beyond Jenbach. North is the Achental which carries a main road over the Achenpass into Germany. The road runs between the Karwendel mountains and the Rofan group. On the main valley is the beautiful

*The Tyrol's dramatic scenery, the Zillertal in winter*

Achensee, a long narrow lake and a favourite spot for windsurfers. South of Jenbach is the Zillertal. Near the head of the valley is Zell am Ziller where a road goes left to climb up into the lovely hanging Gerlos valley and then continues over the Gerlos Pass 507m (1,663ft) into Salzburg Province.

Higher up the valley is Mayrhofen, which stands at the confluence of four valleys coming down from the Zillertal Alps.

Over the Gerlos Pass and down to Mittersill a main road goes south to the Felbertauern Tunnel. This 5km (3-mile) long tunnel has opened up the beautiful valleys of the East Tyrol to tourists and is open all year round.

A road goes down to Lienz before swinging east then north into Carinthia for one of the most spectacular drives of the whole area. From here one may travel north to the village of Heiligenblut which lies on the south slope of the Grossglockner, Austria's highest mountain, and on over a toll road to a height of 2,428m (7,964ft).

The road leads to Zell am See where, by turning back west, one reaches Mittersill, then north to Kitzbühel, a very picturesque winter and summer resort.

From Kitzbühel one can head for Wörgl, back in the main Inn valley, touring gently upstream to Brixlegg and Münster before returning and going on to Kufstein. From here short expeditions can be made to the beautiful lake of Thiersee and round the Kaiser Gebirge (Emperor Mountains) to St Johann in Tyrol, Walschsee and back to Kufstein.

All this is at the eastern end of the Tyrol. In the west the route makes a spectacular entry into the province by way of the Silvretta Strasse. Leaving the motorway at Bludenz and taking the toll road towards Partenen and Galtür, it is almost 100km (62 miles) to Landeck. Caravans are not allowed. The ascent has thirty hairpin bends and starts by following the Montafon valley, through Schruns, at 689m (2,260ft) to the summit of the pass at 2,036m (6,678ft).

From Landeck it is possible to turn back to cross the Arlberg Pass but it is better to turn north near the summit to Zurs and Lech. Lech is at the head of the Lechtal and the River Lech can be followed down to Reutte before coming east again to Ehrwald, a delightful village.

The Fernpass, a valley full of beautiful lakes, leads once more

## PLACENAMES IN AUSTRIA

The visitor to Austria will come across many German words, especially on signs. Many of these are explained in the text, while others are fairly obvious, but to avoid unnecessary repetition the important ones are listed below.

| | | | |
|---|---|---|---|
| *Abtei* | Abbey | *Hoch* | High |
| *Ache* | River | *Horn* | Pointed peak |
| *Alm* | Alpine meadow with a farm–house, now often used as a guesthouse or restaurant | *Joch* | Pass, col |
| | | *Kapelle* | Chapel |
| | | *Kirche* | Church |
| | | *Klamm* | Narrow gorge |
| | | *Klein* | Small |
| | | *Kloster* | Monastery |
| *Alp* | High meadow | *Kogel* | Small hill |
| *Altstadt* | Old quarter of town | *Naturlehrpfad* | Nature trail |
| | | *Naturschutz-gebiet* | Nature reserve |
| *Bach* | Stream | | |
| *Bad* | Spa/bath | *Ober* | Upper, over |
| *Bahnhof* | Railway station | *Rathaus* | Town hall |
| *Berg* | Mountain | *Scharte* | Fissure |
| *Blick* | View | *Schloss* | Castle/palace |
| *Brücke* | Bridge | *See* | Lake |
| *Burg* | Castle/fortification | *Seilschwebe-bahn* | Funicular railway |
| *Dorf* | Village | | |
| *Freibad* | Outdoor swimming pool | *Sesselbahn* | Chair lift |
| | | *Spitze* | Peak |
| *Fremden-verkehrsamt* | Tourist office | *Stadt* | City/town |
| | | *Steig* | Path |
| *Gasthof* | Guesthouse | *Strasse* | Road/street |
| *Gaststätte* | Restaurant | *Tal* | Valley |
| *Gebirge* | Mountain range | *Tierpark* | Zoo |
| *Gross* | Large | *Unter* | Lower, under |
| *Hallenbad* | Indoor swimming pool | *Veste* | Fortress |
| | | *Wald* | Forest |
| *Heimat-museum* | Local museum | *Weg* | Way, path |

*Colourful summer flowers adorn many houses in the Tyrol and Vorarlberg*

*Farming life still carries on in the traditional manner*

into the main Inn valley at Imst. From Landeck over the Arlberg to Reutte and back to Imst, the route has completely encompassed the Lechtaler Alps.

The following chapters will give details of these areas. Do not worry about language difficulties. English is spoken by many of the people and is taught in schools as a primary foreign language from the age of 7. Of course, the larger establishments always make a point of having an English-speaking receptionist. If in doubt, ask. The friendly Austrians delight in being able to explain, or practise their English. Be it the menu, or the best path by which to take in a viewpoint, a friendly cheerful response is assured.

In the Additional Information sections further details are given but most towns and villages have tourist offices where local information is readily available.

It is almost impossible to list all the varied and minor evening entertainments. There is always something available, from a slide show by the local mountain rescue representative, to a Tyrolean shoe platter group. Some only operate in the high season. For instance, at Ehrwald there is a music show with old traditional instruments, but only in the school holidays; in the small village of Telfes, for two weeks each summer, the internationally acclaimed Paraguayan trio 'Los Paraguayos' perform brilliantly but with delightful informality to diners in a local hotel. The local tourist office will have up-to-date times and venues.

The Alpine system of giving times for walks will be adhered to in this guide. Distance is not really relevant to an alpine walk as the ground varies so much and rougher tracks take longer. Times given are for average walkers and allow time for short breaks for taking in the views and for photography. Remember that this is mountain country: ask your overnight host for advice regarding the weather if in doubt. It is always a good idea to carry a small rucksack with a sweater and waterproofs. Bad weather in the Alps usually comes later in the day, so make an early start.

# 1
# *BREGENZERWALD*

---

The Vorarlberg region of Austria is cut off from the main bulk of the country by the Arlberg Pass, hence Vorarlberg or 'before the Arlberg'. Indeed, so separate from the rest of Austria is this region that it almost became part of Switzerland in 1919. The locals claim that the Swiss weather forecast is better and more accurate for them than the Austrian forecast!

Coming south from Lindau in Germany the Austrian border is soon reached. Much traffic speeds along the motorway to the farther reaches of the country, thus missing the Bregenzerwald, which is one of the gems of Austria. The Bregenzerwald is often ignored because it does not contain high mountains: high compared with the grandeur of the Silvretta or the Rätikon, the ranges between the Vorarlberg and Italy. Only a few tops get above the treeline but they make up for it with green rolling hills. From the border with the Tyrol down to Lake Constance (Bodensee) the hills roll gently and with great beauty.

The only way to explore Bregenzerwald is to wander along its deep cut winding valleys through pine forests, where sudden views of tiny farms and villages will reward the patience of a gentle exploratory drive. Sharply pointed as well as rounded peaks, buttressed by wandering grassy ridges, mark the skyline. This is not the country of the alpinist, but is still ideal country for hillwalkers who look for easier and lesser known summits.

The region is basically drained by one major river system, the Bregenzer Ache. Its tributaries carve deep into the shaly mountains of the interior and have, along with the forest and the hand of man in making farmland, determined the geographical character of the Bregenzerwald. The remaining handful of west-flowing streams of the region, also draining into the Rhine, still retain the deeply cut almost V-shaped nature of their brethren. In the south, and marking the region's boundary, is the Grosser Walsertal, its river joining the valley used by the Arlberg section of the west-east Trans-Austrian autobahn. Separated from the Grosser Walsertal by the Zitterklapfen range and the headwaters of the Bregenzer Ache, is the Kleiner (Little) Walsertal. This valley is the odd one out so to speak, part of Austria but completely within the geographical bounds of west Germany, and its river flows eventually into the Danube. The valley has no direct road contact with the rest of Austria, for its headwaters rise in a western arm of the steep Allgäuer Alps. As a result of this inaccessibility, the Kleiner Walsertal has become a toll-free area, an anomaly still found in other parts of Europe similarly cut off from the rest of their country. Quick to take advantage of this concession the inhabitants of the Kleiner Walsertal make a lucrative living from holidaymakers and trippers, mostly from nearby southern Bavaria who come to take advantage of the tax free goods on offer in local shops. However remember the area (though in Austria) uses the Deutschmark, not the Schilling.

Colourful festivals and interesting customs are a major feature of this friendly region. Festivals come in varied forms. The annual Bregenz Music Festival is internationally acclaimed and used by internationally famous orchestras and soloists. The stage is built offshore and is the world's largest stage on a lake. The onshore seating has a capacity of 4,400, extending to 5,000 to accommodate the demand for the production under Jérôme Savary, of *Carmen*. The festival was founded in 1946 when it registered 17,000 guests. Today the figure has risen to over 125,000. The incredible stage is 85m (279ft) and 45m (148ft) in depth, with a cast and crew of about 350 people. Despite the large distance between singer and audience — the singer can be 120m (394ft) away at a level difference of 20m (66ft) — the directional sound system ensures complete clarity for the spectator.

However it is the artistic interpretation of the stage director and stage designer that has contributed to the enormous success of the open-air festival. For instance, the set for *Carmen* had a cast of hundreds of people plus six horses, two donkeys, a sail boat (on the lake), an impressive waterfall, abseiling smugglers de-

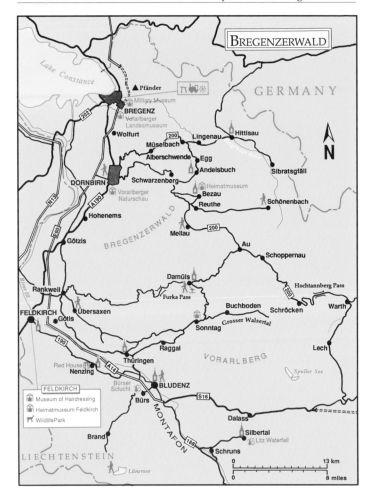

scending 20m (66ft) cliffs, three covered waggons and much use of fireworks, flames and dry ice!

Additionally, in 1980 the Grand Festival Hall was opened adjacent to the open-air theatre with a capacity for 1,750 people. In the event of rain, the outdoor production moves indoor for a limited number of lucky people. Such is the success of the festival, advance booking, up to a year in advance, is advisable. The best

*Martin's Tower, Bregenz*

time to enjoy these concerts or light operas and ballets is on a still evening when the setting sun silhouettes the floating stage and the distant view of the lake and Swiss mountains completes the magic of the setting. The festival is from mid-July to mid-August. Some performances last until close to midnight, so take a jumper etc in case you start to get cold. You will find nearby cafés and bars still open after the concert finishes. If the weather is bad, the concerts are held indoors.

In complete contrast and on a different level, not only geo-graphically but also in meaning, are the religious services held on the summits of mountains throughout the region. The one held on top of the Damülser Mittagspitze, for example, is regularly attended by hundreds of worshippers. The local bishop in all his vestments conducts mass on the narrow summit of the steep-sided grassy mountain.

The local men and women like to wear the regional version of the Austrian national costume at any time, not only on official or festive occasions, but on birthdays or simply for the fun of it. Austrian national dress has the advantage of being practical for everyday wear as well as being attractive. Although there are subtle regional styles (married women from the Bregenzerwald, for instance, wear an elaborately folded scarf) most costumes are based on suede or waterproof loden cloth, spencer jackets for men and wide flounced skirts with embroidered bodices for women (called *dirndl* dresses) made from cotton.

❋    Using **Bregenz**, the regional capital, as a base the villages upstream along the Bregenzer Ache valley can be explored, followed by the minor valleys and towns along the Rhine in a south to north order, on the return to Bregenz.

The pleasant holiday resort of Bregenz sits on a sunny ledge around the eastern extremity of Lake Constance. It was the Romans who first discovered the advantageous site on which Bregenz developed. They built a fortified trading post on their north-south highway between the Alps and what eventually became Germany, probably using the Rhine waterway for the movement of heavy materials. They called their town *Brigantium*, a name which has obviously been gradually changed throughout the intervening centuries to modern Bregenz.

Sheltering the town from cold easterly winter winds are the wooded slopes of the Pfänder mountain 1,063m (3,487ft). The best view of all is from its summit. Take the funicular railway (simply follow signs fo the Pfänderbahn) and try to choose a clear sunny day for your trip. There is an alpine deerpark at the top with demonstrations of birds of prey. Lake Constance stretches westwards in a vast expanse of water over 64km (40 miles) long and up to 13km (8 miles) wide in places. To the right the shoreline is German with the elegant and very old resort town of Lindau connected to the mainland by a narrow causeway. Gently indented bays, all with their formal bathing beaches, stretch into the blue haze of a distant view backed by a hint of the rolling hills of the Black Forest. On the left and across the canalised Rhine which is the border between Austria and Switzerland, is the busy but pretty little Swiss town of Rorschach which looks north across the lake from a wide bay. Further on is Romanshorn with its regular ferry services to and from industrial Friedrichshafen in Germany. Finally Konstanz marks both a frontier and also the outflow of the main lake into the Untersee. Beyond the lesser lake the Rhine takes over again, navigable with the exception of the Rhine Falls at Schaffhausen (literally meaning 'Boat Houses'), all the way to the North Sea.

Further round to the left the view is along the deep trough of the Rhine valley southwards past Liechtenstein, a principality with close political links to Switzerland and yet geographically within Austria. On a really clear day the snow-clad peaks of the Swiss Alps mark the southern boundary of this wonderful view, said by many to be one of the finest in Europe. The view is complemented by the compact grouping of buildings in the oldest part of Bregenz (the Alte Stadt). The attractive houses, still partly within the remains of the thirteenth-century ramparts, sit at the foot of the Pfänder mountain, blending well with the 'new town' which follows the lakeshore as far as the Bregenzer Ache, the main river of this region. Across the river and on low lying ground between it and the Rhine canal are the small industrial towns of Hard, Lauterach and Wolfurt, occupying the only space where modern expansion is possible.

Boats carrying the flags of Germany and Switzerland, as well as Austria, regularly leave the busy harbour to the north of Bregenz Bahnhof, the main railway station, and visit towns all around the lake. Remember to take your passport and appropriate currency if embarking on a cruise along Lake Constance, as it is not always convenient to change money at the port of call.

Bregenz has a good shopping centre, but goods are expensive and it is cheaper to go to nearby Germany. Incidentally if it is groceries or alcohol you need, proceed to Lindau and just before reaching the town look out for the Aldi store on the right. It takes some beating in terms of prices! If you would prefer to buy fuel with a credit card instead of cash (virtually impossible in this end of Austria) fill up in Germany. If you would like to buy some of the lovely Austrian clothes (particularly womens), you may have a surprise in some of the villages which have a reasonable range at prices cheaper than Bregenz (eg Hittisau).

The swimming pools and sports complex beyond the Opera House at Bregenz is recommended and also caters for small children. On the outskirts of the town is the Cistercian monastery of Mehrerau. It is worth trying to make an appointment to be shown around here as only the church is usually open to the public. It has a magnificent library with many early books.

The church itself is modern, the previous building having been sold to build the harbour extension at Lindau. In the undercroft you can see the remains of a Roman church. The Romans had a town here, situated above the main road to Lauterach (Römerstrasse). The harbour in Roman times was where this street meets Rathausstrasse. This corner is where you can wander off up Maurachgasse which leads up to the Old Town (Altstadt). This is a charming and quiet backwater which is dominated by the Martinsturm, a large tower built in 1602 with the largest onion dome in Europe, dating from the early Baroque period. Among the buildings in this area is the former Rathaus of 1662.

The Vorarlberger Landesmuseum in Kornmarkt (off Rathausstrasse) has an interesting, if somewhat sanitised collection of items covering Vorarlberg from the old Stone Age period (including a magnificent mammoth's tusk from this period). Roman Bregenz is well represented and there are a couple of rooms representing a sitting-room from a Montafon farmhouse and a Bludenz Bürgermaster's house. Although all the signs are in German it is possible to understand most things and a visit is recommended. The top floor has a lot of early religious wooden carvings and a good collection of paintings by Angelika Kaufman (the Vorarlberg artist who was born in 1741). The museum (like most commercial properties) has the irritating practice of

*A quiet corner of the old town in Bregenz*

*There are flower beds all along the lakeside at Bregenz*

closing at lunchtime.

The Roman town lay above Römerstrasse, the main road out of town to Dornbirn. Unfortunately virtually the whole of the site, including the Forum lies under high-class housing in Ölrinstrasse. There is a villa site preserved although there are no signs to it and it is not marked on town maps. It is a large site, completely unattended and becoming overgrown. The villa was a square building with a central courtyard. It may be found between the end of Bahnhofstrasse and Klostergasse, adjacent to the slip road to the City Tunnel. A footpath runs along the edge of the site between the two streets.

Bregenz also has a casino. If you happen to be in the town for Silvester night (New Year's Eve), take a stroll to the harbour just before midnight and await a pleasant surprise. On Christmas Eve, the passenger ferry boat meets others from Switzerland and Germany in the middle of the lake for a short service complete with Santa Claus who gives the children a little present.

Bregenz comes into its own in summer when the flowers decorating the beds of its spacious promenade are at their best. Regattas and informal sailing competitions are held on the lake throughout the summer season and the lakeside concerts enjoy one of the finest and most imaginative auditoriums possible.

Until recently there was a little railway which wound its way from Bregenz to Bezau, climbing about 253m (830ft) in the space of about 30km (19 miles). The line hugged the river for most of the way, mirroring its tight bends as it climbed through the narrow gorge. However, there is still a short section of track between  Bezau and Bersbuch where a narrow gauge steam train runs daily trips. On either hand are pretty villages and neat farms within a colourful tapestry of meadows set against a backcloth of dark green forest.

The village of **Buch** sits high above the valley and was a good half mile from its station, but neighbouring **Alberschwende** had no rail connections. What it does have is a useful chairlift to the top of the Bruggelekopf, a delightful pine-clad mountain (1,182m, 3,877ft), the focal point of at least four easy-to-follow and clearly marked woodland paths. An enjoyable day could be spent by driving to Buch then taking the quiet lane which winds its way, more or less south, to Alberschwende with its welcoming cafés and *Gasthofe*. Take the chairlift to the top of the Bruggelekopf and descend to the east then south-east by way of the Gasthof Alpenrose where a winding hill road leads down to Egg.

Beyond Alberschwende, the main road descends down into the valley of the Bregenzerache (look to the left at the bottom of the hill to see the old narrow railway line above the road) before climbing up to Egg (where the right turn goes to Schwartzenberg, see below). Egg is a rather large village with three supermarkets and two shop developments either side of the cross roads. Above Sutterlüty's supermarket is a rather large clothes shop with many examples of traditional dresses plus loden wear which is manu-factured here. The left turn goes off to Grossdorf, past the local brewery which produces a light and pleasant tasting beer. **Grossdorf** is a small, pretty village with a road off to the right which climbs up onto the alps above the River Suberache with views across to Sibratsgfäll. The through road proceeds to Lingenau and a horse drawn carriage operates between the two villages allowing you to observe the scenery at one horse-power.

The name **Egg** always amuses children. It has nothing to do with the products of hens but is a local name probably connected with an old word for a ridge, the true meaning lost in the mists of time. There are several villages and hamlets with Egg somewhere in their title in the surrounding district. The village sits astride the main river, joined here by two minor streams both of which will reward a day's quiet exploration. By-roads follow the wooded high ground to remote villages like **Hittisau**, a scattered rural hamlet grouped around its white Baroque onion-domed church. Opposite the church in Hittisau, the road bears to the left and starts to leave the village. Take the right turn upon reaching a crossroads and drop down towards the River Bolgenach. Just before reaching the river is the village swimming pool. There are twin pools with a pool for small children all out of doors, plus a café, a lawn for sun bathing, lockers etc. Infact it is typical of many found in the area. Cross the bridge and turn right (upstream). The road climbs up to a small lake (the Leckner See) and ends at a tiny chapel and farmhouse only just in Austria. The valley is beautiful and very isolated. There is a car park a few hundred yards before the lake if you fancy a stroll up the road. It is possible to hire cycles in Hittisau and there is an outdoor swimming pool.

Beyond Hittisau, the road starts to climb up towards the Balderschwangertal, a long flattish valley which straddles the

*Replacing the wooden shingles on the church dome at Lingenau, near Hittisau, in the Bregenzerwald*

*Sibratsgfäll in the Bregenzerwald* ⇒

border with Germany. A turn off this road to the right leads up to another valley with the pretty little village of **Sibratsgfäll**. It has a small restaurant and adjacent shop just before the church. The village is well off the beaten track probably because cars can not proceed beyond the border. The German side is a conservation area. The valley splits just beyond the village. The river to the south flows down from Schönenbach (see below) but there is no connecting road. The other valley from Sibratsgfäll is the Hirschgundtal with a footpath up to the Polus Wasserfall. The large waterfall is actually on the Austrian/German border and is visible from just before you reach Sibratsgfäll.

If you have time to stay a while in this area, you can hire bikes from the shop and proceed over the border for a couple of kilometres. Take your passport but expect the border to be unmanned. Upon reaching a couple of houses you can continue down the magnificent valley with only an occasional car. Alternatively, you can turn right downhill to the river and recross back into Austria. Ahead and to the left is the waterfall, reached by turning left at a farmhouse. If time permits, proceed up through the wood above the waterfall having left your bike at the bottom (theft is virtually unheard of). Eventually the waymarked path leaves the wood and climbs up to two mountain huts. It is a little over 2 hours to the upper hut but the views are memorable. Ahead is the peak of Hirscheck at 1,919m (6,294ft) and the waymarked path continues up to the top. Allow 4 hours to get there from your bike. The area to the south from the peak (across the Löwental) is an incredible sight of large humps and depressions in shattered limestone stretching across to the top of the ski lift from the Kleiner Walsatal and the pyramid-shaped mountain of Hoherifen, rising to 2,230m (7,314ft). As with many of the upper valleys, it is a mass of alpine flowers in the summer once you leave the tree line.

An interesting surprise lies hidden in the wood at Ifenblick. Climbing the road out of Sibratsgfäll towards Hittisau, as one reaches the top, a road leads off to the left (behind the guesthouse) to the top of the ski lift. There is a tiny foot bridge opposite the ski lift and just beyond it, by a small house. Take this footpath along a line of paving stones to the local *Moorbad* or peat bath. There are two peaty water pools and a disgusting looking, but shallow, peat bath to lie in! These are surrounded by a wicket fence and there is a shower. They are free and the locals swear they are good for easing away aches and strains.

As with most alpine villages, the best time to visit is in early summer before haymaking when the meadow flowers are at their best. Some of the meadows here and up to Sibratsgfäll are full of the snow bell in spring. It is a white bell-type flower with a yellow tip known as the 'schneeglockner'. It is usually followed by masses of cowslips. Another road from Egg leads to Gross-dorf, and to **Ittensberg**, where there is a guest house and the delightful little Fatima chapel.

Continue south, upstream along the main river, where the road moves away from the river in order to reach the area of habitation. At this point the farms and meadowland tend to be low lying and prone to flooding so all buildings are well away from any danger. **Andelsbuch** is next, a friendly little place where time seems to stand still. Again, the focal point is its white walled church with a tower capped by the ubiquitous onion dome. Paragliding and hang-gliding are available and there are eight ski lifts. The tourist information centre can make reservations and supply you with more information.

Between Andelsbuch and Bezau a beautiful road goes off to the right, leading to Schwarzenberg and Bodele before twisting its way down to Dornbirn. Bodele is just a hamlet with a hotel but Schwarzenberg is a proper little village. It is often missed by tourists and has a charming centre of several very old farms, a preserved farmhouse and a museum dedicated to the famous artist Angelika Kaufmann (1741-1807) who was born here.

After a temporary narrowing, the valley broadens and **Bezau** marks the former terminus of the little train from Bregenz. The rolling stock has been preserved and you can take a steam ride as  far as Bersbuch. You can return by train or walk back via Bezegg ($1\,^3/_4$ hours) There is a small exhibition of old photographs of the line in the old station buildings. From the eastern end of the village street a short cablecar ride reaches the Niedere ridge where the walking is ideal for all types of mountain lovers. To the east, the ridge is followed by a clear path marked by the standard  red/white splashes to the Winterstade peak (1,877m, 6,156ft) one of the highest points in this part of the Bregenzerwald. Easier paths, again well signposted and waymarked, wander down the forested ridge back to Bezau, although an extension can be made

*Bezau*

*Au*

*Rankweil, at the foot of the Furka Pass road*

to the Gasthof Sonderlach close to the middle station of the cablecar. Especially on hot days, this option is likely to be the most popular part of an enjoyable day in the mountains.

A little further on, a road off to the left leads to Reuthe, Bizau and **Schönenbach**. The latter is about as far as the road is worth following, though it does go on to some farms. There are two guest houses at Schönenbach and some delightful walks in a lovely mix of woods and meadows. One of these goes to a large waterfall. Again springtime finds this area full of alpine flowers. This valley is really off the beaten track and worth investigating.

The main valley route now goes through a series of villages with 'au' as part of their name. First comes **Mellau** where the lower crags of the Hangspitze rise steeply above the wooded valley sides and make the 1,746m (5,727ft) mountain appear to be higher than it actually is. South of the village a cablecar could take you to the Rosstelle Alm, a high corrie developed for winter skiing but perfectly suitable for summer strolling, picnicking or enjoying the mountain flowers. A zigzag path leads to the  Hofstatten Haus, an interesting alpine hut set just above the treeline beneath the rocky slopes of the Ranisfluh ridge. Mellau is a useful place to stop off for refreshments and is bypassed by the main road.

**Au** marks the junction of two roads once more important than today. Beyond Au there is a fair spread of dwellings and several hamlets and this green and pleasant area tempts one to linger. However, continue along the valley route as far as **Schröcken**, a tiny village which makes a suitable base for high-level mountain rambling in the Allgauer and Lechtaler Alps. Above the village, the road climbs in a series of tight hairpin bends to the Hochtannberg Pass (1,679m, 5,507ft) before dropping down into Lechtal and Warth where it divides, one road following the Lech downstream to Reutte and the German frontier and the other upstream to Lech and across the Flexenpass to join the Arlberg Pass road.

A little way along the main road from Au is **Schoppernau**, a colourful place complete with all the amenities for a mountain holiday, including a swimming pool and also the bottom station of a chairlift to the summit of the Diedamskopf (2,090m, 6,855ft), the start of an exciting high-level walk well within the capabilities of anyone used to hillwalking and one of the largest chairlifts in Austria. There is a restaurant at the top and family discount.  Several paths lead down from the mountain and a route should be chosen from a local map — *Freytag and Bernt's 1:100,000 Bregenzerwald* is ideal. A strong party could return by way of the Schwarzwasser Haus, an attractive alpine hut offering excellent refreshments, or if you want an easier walk, then try the footpath beneath the Falzerkopf to the Diedemsalm, again offering refreshment.

The other road from Au runs to the south-west above the left bank of the Argenbach stream to Damüls and the Furka Pass (1,760m, 5,773ft) before dropping down to Rankweil in the Rhine valley. The steep road is narrow in places and sits on a rocky ledge, but the problem of passing other vehicles is avoided by the simple expedient of a tidal flow system. By this method vehicles run in one direction only during advertised times, the flow being reversed during alternate periods. The system works very well, but relies upon the patience of all road users: it only needs one thoughtless motorist to drive the wrong way along a particularly narrow part of the road to throw the whole operation in chaos.

The only village of any size on the Furka Pass road is **Damüls**, the highest in the Bregenzerwald. This is a popular ski resort in winter with seven ski lifts and a ski school, but far from being  exploited as a mountain holiday village in summer, although it is a centre for mountaineering in the Vorarlberg. Two chairlifts take the effort out of climbing the steepest hillsides and strategically sited *Gasthofe* and alpine huts make Damüls an ideal centre for a real away-from-it-all mountain holiday. The main lift is sometimes closed in summer. If you are not in the mood for walking but fancy a short stop, take the road which climbs the hill adjacent to the lift to the Wallisgarten Gasthof and its sun terrace where the views are magnificent. The road is surfaced to this  point only.

The shaly nature of the subsoil of the grassy mountains on either side of the Furka Pass have created an excellent growing media for a wide range of alpine flowers, their bright colours tempting even the most blasé mountain walker to stop and admire their beauty. Hopefully, he or she will only take photographs because picking alpine flowers frequently kills the parent plant and it is also illegal to pick many of the species found growing in the Alps.

The Damülser Mittagspitze is the venue for an annual Mass, taken usually by the local bishop. If you stand on the narrow grassy summit in a strong breeze you may try to imagine the poor man's difficulty in keeping his feet on the ground when the wind fills his vestments like a parachute!

Damüls church has long acted as a beacon for travellers on the Furka Pass road. It sits a little aloof from the modern hotels and *Gasthöfe* of the village, high above a sharp right-hand bend in the road, the bright red onion-dome topping the slender tower visible for miles. Inside is the Baroque splendour of its altar illuminated by the narrow, high-placed windows set in bare whitewashed walls. The old part of the village also has some interesting wooden houses.

By using either of the chairlifts, a whole new world of easy high-level walking opens across the hillsides and grassy ridges surrounding Damüls. Strategically placed alpine huts and *Gasthofe* provide sustenance and short, often level, tracks lead to neighbouring villages.

**Fontanella** is such a spot sitting to the south on a sunny terrace high above the Grosser Walsertal. The track which links it to Damüls is flat and wooded but to reach it by car you must join the magnificent new road just below Damüls, crossing the valley and climbing up to **Faschina**. The section across the valley is in the form of a gallery, but below Faschina the road has not yet been improved and hairpin bends lead down beyond the Faschina hotels to Fontanella. More hairpins lead down from Fontanells to the main valley, the Grosser Walsertal, which, despite its narrowness, is worthy of a visit. The road is a cul-de-sac so traffic is rarely a problem. The valley gets its name from some of its early inhabitants. In the thirteenth century the Montfort family became vassals of Hugo of Tubingen. By the end of the century the Montforts (Hugo had adopted the name) controlled what is now the Vorarlberg. They were responsible for opening up the country and bringing in people from the Swiss canton of Wallis. Most of them settled in the Grosser Walsertal which is named after them.

Climbing up the valley there is the hamlet of **Buchboden** and a few kilometres beyond is the head of the valley with only one or two farms. The last one is the Metzgertobel Alm, almost at the head wall.

*Damüls is popular for winstersports*

*The Damüls area is also popular for touring in the summer*

From the valley head paths lead upward into the foothills of the Lechtaler Alps to the south and the Zitterklapfen range to the north. The two main alpine huts are the Goppinger and Biberacher, but many of the small hill farms add to their income by selling refreshments. Lower down the valley is mostly forest, but farms and attractive hamlets line the road and side tracks. Going down the valley the first hamlet is **Sonntag**. This small village has a local museum and a cablecar climbing the south side of the valley. Two kilometres down the valley there is a turning left to **Raggal**. There is a camp site at Plazera, just before Raggal is reached, and a turning left to Marul, a very small hamlet. Raggal is a pleasant little village with the local reservoir as an added attraction. The dam wall is 48m (157ft) high. The parish church dates from the fourteenth century. There are plenty of footpaths and with the nearby villages of Ledesch, with its interesting church, and Thüringen, with its two churches, the area can fill in quite a lot of time. The parish church at **Thüringen** has a silver monstrance and a Rococo organ, and the St Anna church dates from the sixteenth century. Nearby are two ruined castles — Joran and Blumberg, dating from the thirteenth century.

The next little group of villages, **Duns, Rons, Schnifis** and **Schlins**, offer bathing at the Fallersee and cablecars up to the heights of the Dunserberg. Near Schlins there is yet another ruined castle, the Jagdberg, dating between the thirteenth and the sixteenth centuries. Also for the odd wet day there is an indoor swimming pool. **Übersaxen** is noted for the lovely walks round about the village.

At the other side of the Au to Schrocken road lies the Kleiner Walsertal, but this is completely inaccessible by road from Austria. A strong party could, however, easily walk over the Hochalp Pass from the top of the Hochtannberg Pass, having reached the latter by postbus. The path leads round the dramatic western slopes of the rocky Widderstein (2,533m, 8,308ft) and reaches the Kleiner Walsertal road end at Baad. **Mittelberg** is about 3km (2 miles) further down the valley and, depending on time, a profitable extension could be made to the duty free shops. But remember that anything you buy will have to be carried and liquor weighs heavy after a while no matter how cheap it may be in the shops!

All the major towns in the region, with the exception of **Bludenz** lie in the Rhine valley. This lovely old town is at the foot of the Arlberg Pass and its centre is closed to traffic which uses the bypass. It is a bustling little town with a modern shopping centre but also some quiet shopping precincts under ancient archways and a lovely old square which is taken over by the town band on highdays and holidays. The town has four churches, including the seventeenth-century hospital chapel, two swimming pools, a museum, and a castle. Local legend has it that unicorns still roam in nearby woods. There is also a cable car to Mittersberg at 1,400m (4,592ft).

The Montafon railway runs between Bludenz and Schruns at hourly intervals throughout the day from 6am to 10pm, with occasional steam trains. This is a useful little railway if one wishes to leave the car behind for a change.

Continuing on the road towards Feldkirch, Nenzing dates back to AD850 and is an interesting village with two churches dating from the fifteenth century. The Red House is a wooden house from the seventeenth century, said to be impregnated with bulls' blood to give it colour. Nenzing also claims the most modern heated swimming pool in the Vorarlberg. There is a splendid walk taking in the ruined Schloss Ramschwag and giving a good view over the village.

Nenzing lies at the foot of the Gamperdonatal, a gloriously beautiful valley cutting deep into the Alps. Near the head of the valley lies Nenzinger Himmel (*himmel* means heaven). Here, deep in the Rhätikon group of mountains, only 1km ($^1/_2$ mile) from the Liechtenstein border and just over 2km (1 mile) from the Swiss border, this lovely hamlet nestles in dramatically beautiful surroundings. Here is the tiny chapel of St Rochus and an old watermill. Along the path to the Gufel Alm is the Stuberfall (waterfall) and, not far from the village, the Rotes Brunnele (Red Spring). Fortunately for this peaceful area, but unfortunately for the tourist, the road is closed to traffic. Access is by way of a fleet of yellow and white minibuses from Nenzing, which are not cheap, or by foot along the 12km ($7^1/_2$ mile) long valley.

The next valley, the Brandnertal, can be reached on foot from Nenzinger Himmel or by bus from the main valley. The last bus stop up the valley is right at the road head just about a kilometre from the Douglas hut but 400m (1,300ft) lower, so be prepared for a climb which is worth the effort.

Surpassing the beauty of the Brandnertal, and only reached by a cablecar at 1,970m (6,461ft) is the **Lünersee.** The lake is about 2km (1 miles) long and 1$^1$/$_2$km (1 mile) wide. There is a good footpath all the way round and spectacular scenery. To work up an appetite for lunch one could walk round the west bank of the lake and go up to the Totalphütte at 2,385m (7,823ft). Here, the tiny Totalpsee sits like a jewel set in the alpine scenery. A little further west, the other side of the ridge, is the Brand glacier. Here another small lake is joined to the Totalpsee by a pipeline under the mountains. Another pipeline feeds water from the Lunersee down to the Montafon valley and the hydro-electric works at Latschau.

The road to the Brandnertal from the main valley is opposite Bludenz. **Bürs** is the first village, still quite low. Here, the main river of the valley, the Ill, is forced through a gorge, the Burser Schlucht. The village has a heated open-air swimming pool. Nearby, **Tschengla** is a quiet village sitting on a sun terrace up above the main valley.

*A local band concert in Bludenz*

**Bürserberg** is the next village, the first glimpse of which causes many people to stop and reach for a camera as the views of the church are very good. **Brand** is the main tourist area of the valley. Here, there is a daily programme of entertainments, a number of hotels, and chairlifts up to the western heights above the village. There is a cablecar to the Lünersee with a circular walk around the lake at 2,000m (6,560ft) surrounded by a ring of high mountains.

Go on from Nenzing, via road 190, where on the edge of the ancient flood plain of the Rhine, close by the border with Liechtenstein, is **Feldkirch**, a romantic old town which boasts, of all things, a Museum of Hairdressing, tracing the fads and fashions throughout the centuries. The town dates from a first mention as *Veldkirchun* in the year AD830. Parts of the existing town are medieval and, being strategically placed Feldkirch once controlled movement from the Rhine into Austria. Powerful barons controlled this trade route from Schloss Schattenburg, which is open to the public and which houses a local museum. There are no less than six interesting churches in the town and four towers dating from the thirteenth to the sixteenth century. There is also much more to see, and the information office in the Schlosser Gasse have leaflets giving further details. There is a nearby zoo and a camp site by the river to the north-west.

Travelling north, pass through the pleasant villages of Rankweil (with its lovely nineteenth-century church set on a rocky outcrop), Götzis and Hohenems to reach **Dornbirn**. This is an important little town, the centre of one of Austria's major textile regions. Each year a textile show is held when most of the top fashion designers vie with each other to produce the latest styles for the coming season. The show usually coincides with the Bregenz Music Festival. The old town centre is not spoilt, however, as industry is relegated to the outskirts. There are some good guest houses and restaurants, many sports facilities, an exhibition centre and a shopping centre. You can visit the Vorarlberger Naturschau (Natural History Museum) or the forest swimming pool which is situated on the bank of the Dornbirner Ach river. A short cablecar ride to Karren from the south-eastern outskirts of Dornbirn reaches a series of gentle wooded ridges scattered with conveniently spaced mountain restaurants. There is ample scope across the broad ridges and hilltops for several days of easy walking. The choice is almost unlimited but, as an example, try the route which connects a series of paths, south-west from Karren by way of the Gasthof Schwarzenberg, then on to the Emser hut and eventually reach the main valley at Klaus. This is roughly 16m (10 miles) in length but has easy forest and hilltop walking for most of its length.

Near Dornbirn a small road leads beyond the cable car to Karren through a wooded valley with saw mills and textile factories to the Rappenlochschlucht. Here the river has cut a channel through a very narrow ravine. It seems to attract few visitors, which is no reason for not taking the trouble to find it! It is quite spectacular and rewards the effort.

North of Dornbirn look out (high on the right) for the twin towers of the church at **Bildstein** near to Wolfurt. It is worth taking the car up to it. The view is magnificent and there is a pleasant *Gasthof* uphill from it. The church dates from 1663 and is surrounded by several rather old houses.There is a nice restaurant at the side of the church in an hotel, with a *Gasthof* nearby as an alternative for a quiet summers evening. The road from Wolfurt climbs steeply and is narrow in places. There is a small private zoo at the bottom of the hill next to a factory.

To complete the circuit of the Bregenzerwald the series of south-west flowing river valleys which drain into the Bregenzer Ache are well worth exploring. None of the broad intervening ridges are high or steep. Pretty farms make use of the sunny situation and many a happy hour can be spent wandering close to the German border along lanes and trackways rarely visited by anyone other than locals.

## Additional Information

### Bregenz: Places Of Interest

**Folklore Evening, Folklore and Dancing**
Gasthaus Gösserbräu
Anton-Schneider-Strasse 1
Entrance 75
Open: 8.30pm.

**Military Museum**
In the Martinsturm, Alstadt
Open: from Easter to October.

**Vorarlbeger Landesmuseum**
Kornmarktplatz
Open: 9am-12noon and 2-5pm.
Closed Mondays.

## *Bregenz: Useful Information*

**AUTOMOBILE AND TOURING CLUB**
Brosswaldenstrasse
☎ 44378

Rossmähder 2
☎ (05572) 23692

ARBÖ
Lastenstrasse 5
☎ 38100

**BICYCLE HIRE**
Drissner
Rheinstrasse 64
☎ 36336

Kaufmann Roman
Brielgasse 40
☎ 37589
Bicycle hire is available from May onwards at the lakeside and cycle touring maps are available from the tourist office.

**BREGENZ FESTIVAL**
Brochures and tickets are available from:
Bregenzer Festspiele Gmbh
Platz der Wiener Symphoniker
6900 Bregenz
☎ 49200

**CAR GARAGES**
Parking House GWL
Am Leutbühel
☎ 43737

Hotel Bodensee
Kornmarktstrasse 22
☎ 42300

Hotel z Grauen Bären
Reichsstrasse 8
☎ 42823

Hypobank
Hypopassage 1
☎ 4140

**CAR HIRE**
AVIS
Am Brand 2
☎ 42222

Säly and König
Albergstrasse 135
☎ 31115

Hertz
Landesreisebüro
Jahnstrasse 13-15
☎ 4911

**GUIDES**
The Vorarlberger Landesreisebüro
Jahnstrasse 13-15
A-6900 Bregenz
☎ (0)5574/4911-0

**HOSPITAL**
Municipal Hospital
Carl-Pedenz-Strasse 2
☎ 4010

Mehrerau Sanatorium
Mehrerauer Strasse 72
☎ 31240

Emergency Hospital
Josef-Huter-Strasse 12
☎ 250312 or 49010

**PHARMACY**
Bahnhofsapotheke
Bahnhofstrasse 25
☎ 42942

Löwenapotheke
Rathaustrasse 15
☎ 42040

Brückenapotheke
Achgasse 65 (behind Ford Wehinger)
☎ 37800

St Gebhard Apotheke
Heldendankstrasse 42
☎ 31798

Stadtapotheke
Kirchstrasse 7
☎ 42102

POLICE
Bahnhofstrasse 43
☎ 42021
Emergency calls ☎ 122

POST OFFICE
Main Post Office
Seestrasse 5
☎ 49000

Schendlingen Post Office
Schendlinger Strasse 10
☎ 31699

Vorkloster Post Office
Vorklostergasse 37
☎ 42200

TOURIST INFORMATION
Anton-Schneider-Strasse 4a
A-6900 Bregenz
☎ (05574) 43391

## Other Places Of Interest

### Bezau
*Heimatmuseum Bezau*
Verkehrsamt Bezau
Open: Tuesday, Thursday,
Saturday 2-4pm; Wednesday
10am-12noon.

### Bludenz
*Heimatmuseum Bludenz*
Obere Tor
Open: Tuesday to Saturday 10am-
12noon, 3-6pm; Sunday 10am-
12noon, 3-6pm; Sunday 10am-
12noon.

### Dornbirn
*Vorarlberger Naturschau
(Natural History Museum)*
Marktstrasse 33
Open: daily 9am-12noon, 2-5pm.

*Forest Swimming Pool*
On the bank of the Dornbirner Ach
16 Gütlestrasse
Open: May to mid-September 9am-
7.30pm.

### Feldkirch
*Heimatmuseum Feldkirch*
Schattenburg
Open: daily 9am-5pm, except
Wednesdays when it is open for
visiting groups only.

*Wildlife Park*
Open: daily 9am-5pm.

### Hard
*Mittelweiher Castle*
Open: Tuesday and Thursday in
July and August. Conducted tour
10am or by appointment.

### Hohenems
*Annual 'Schubertiade' Music Festival*
Concerts actually held in Feldkirch
at either the Monforthaus or the
Konservatoriumssaal. The
programme is not confined to the
music of Schubert. Details are
always available at Bregenz tourist
office. For information and box
office contact:
Schweizer Strasse 1
Postfach 100
A-6845 Hohenems
☎ (05576) 2091

*Jewish Museum*
Schweizer Strasse 1
Open: Bank Holidays 10am-5pm.

## *Tourist Information Centres*

**Alberschwende**
A-6861
☎ (5579) 4233

**Andelsbuch**
A-6866
☎ (5512) 2565

**Au**
A-6883
☎ (5515) 2288

**Bezau**
A-6870
☎ (5514) 2295

**Bludenz**
A-6700
☎ (5552) 62170

**Brand**
A-6708
☎ (5559) 555

**Bregenz**
A-6900
☎ (5552) 8127, 8120

**Buch**
A-6960
☎ (5579) 8295

**Bürserberg**
A-6700
☎ (5552) 63317

**Damüls**
A-6884
☎ (5510) 253

**Dornbirn**
A-6850
☎ (5572) 62188

**Egg**
A-6863
☎ (5512) 2426

**Feldkirch**
A-6800
☎ (5522) 23467

**Fontanella / Faschina**
A-6733
☎ (5554) 5357, 5223

**Hittisau**
A-6952
☎ (5513) 6354

**Hohenems**
A-6845
☎ (5576) 4647

**Mellau**
A-6881
☎ (5518) 2203

**Mittelberg** (Kleiner Walsertal)
A-6993
☎ (5517) 5114-0

**Nenzing**
A-6710
☎ (5525) 2215

**Raggal / Marul**
A-6741
☎ (5553) 345

**Schnifis**
A-6822
☎ (5524) 8515

**Schoppernau**
A-6886
☎ (5515) 2495

**Schröcken**
A-6888
☎ (5519) 267

**Sonntag / Buchboden**
A-6731
☎ (5554) 5292

# 2

# MONTAFON, ARLBERG AND THE LECHTAL

It is about 72km (45 miles) from Bludenz to Landeck, with the summit of the Bierlerhöhe Pass being reached about halfway. The road is generally closed by snow from November to May and has a toll which is collected beyond Partenen. The Tyrol is reached at the pass which is at 2,036m (6,678ft).

Near Landeck a left turn goes back up to the Arlberg Pass on road 315. Crossing the Arlberg back into the region of Vorarlberg is the most convenient route into the famous Lechtal, via the town of Lech where the river Lech is joined. The route continues down the magnificent Lechtal to Reutte, almost on the German border.

From Reutte it is possible to cross the border into Germany to visit the castles at **Schwangau.** There are two campsites on the lakeside, and two castles. Hohenschwangau is the original castle and was once a home. Neuschwanstein is the fairytale castle built by Ludwig of Bavaria. Its interior was never completed as Ludwig met a sad end, drowned in the nearby lake. However, the exterior is a fantastic sight. The spires and turrets make a fascinating sight when viewed either from the valley or from higher up the many paths through the woods. Car parking is in the valley and the walk up the driveway takes almost half an hour. There are horse drawn carriages which travel almost to the top. English speaking guides are available on request at no extra cost.

From an approach past Lake Constance through Lindau and Bregenz take the motorway to Bludenz and follow it until the signs for Schruns appear. Leave the motorway and take the road into the Montafon valley, signposted Partenen and Galtür. The Silvretta Road is closed to caravans, no doubt due to its thirty hairpin bends and 1,000m (3,280ft) of ascent. However, it is possible to camp in the main valley and tour the Silvretta Road, returning over the Arlberg.

The Montafon valley is very pleasant and fairly heavily populated. After St Anton and off the main road through the valley is **Vandans**, the self-proclaimed 'Flower Capital of Europe'. **Tschagguns** and **Schruns**, within a little over a kilometre of each other, are the next places reached. The ancient village centre of Schruns, the main town in the valley, offers a very pleasant stroll and the Dorfstrasse is closed to motor traffic which enhances the pleasure. It is not a fashionable place in the tourist sense but has some good skiing in the winter and splendid views of the Ratikon group to the west. Both villages are winter and summer resorts.

Just before the next town there is a turning south to **Gargellen**, a tiny Alpine village at 1,480m (4,854ft). **St Gallenkirch** is a picturesque town with the usual winter facilities, while **Gaschurn** is the next little place on route, a popular winter sports resort. Local guides will take parties on mountaineering or skiing tours on the Silvretta or Ferwall while the less energetic can fish, ride or just stroll through the woods of the lower slopes.

The valley now has a more alpine look and from the village of **Partenen**, the ascent proper begins. Partenen is a pleasant village, lying at 1,050m (3,444ft) and there is very good skiing. Just beyond the village the Silvretta High Alpine Road begins; this is actually a private road belonging to the power company and there is a toll. The road curves and bends for 24km (15 miles) and climbs 1,000m (3,280ft) to the Bielerhöhe Pass at 2,036m (6,678ft).

One of the large power plants is at Partenen, another higher up the valley. Water is piped down from the lakes and dams at considerable pressure. Both plants were opened before World War II but enlarged afterwards when artificial lakes were built.

Vermunt-Stausee, the first lake, at 1,743m (5,717ft), allows a pause in the climb. The summit of the pass, the Bielerhöhe (2,036m, 6,678ft) is a natural stopping place. A large hotel is a base for mountain expeditions and for spring skiing in the Silvretta Mountains. It is possible to walk along the crest of the dam which is 431m (1,414ft) long and 80m (262ft) high. The mountain peaks to the south form the border with Switzerland: the highest mountain in view is the Piz Buin, 3,316m (10,876ft) high.

On the eastern shore of the lake is the Tyrol border. Downhill

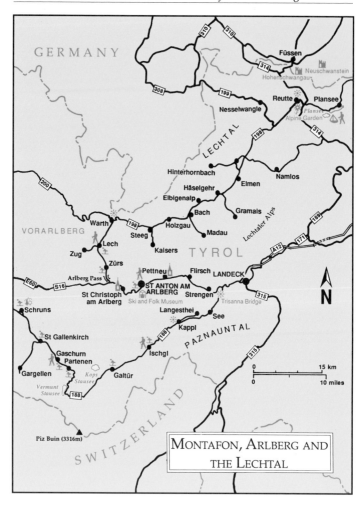

MONTAFON, ARLBERG AND
THE LECHTAL

to the east is the grassy dell of Kleinvermunt leading down to the Paznaun valley and the Trisanna river. **Galtür** is the first hamlet with five winter chair lifts and an indoor swimming pool. There is a bus service from Landeck up the main valley to Galtür.

For an alpine walk from Galtür go south of the village up the **Jamtal**. Involving 332m (1,089ft) of ascent it is a good safe walk up to the Jamtalhutte, an alpine hut more like an inn. Return the

*Vandans, famous for
its flowers*

*Gargellen, in the
Montafon valley*

same way. The time required to reach the hut is about $2^1/_2$ hours. There is parking space at the Scheibalm.

The next village down the Paznauntal is **Ischgl**, and is below the tree line which was reached on the way down from Galtür. Built on a slight spur and below the village church, it is most attractive, lying at 1,377m (4,517ft). It is the largest village in the valley, and is regarded as a health resort in summer. It is, of course, a skiing centre in winter, while fishing and riding are also available. Both villages have tourist offices at which to check exact locations and times.

There is a cable car which can quickly whisk one to a height of 2,612m (8,567ft). It is possible to walk down from here but at this height it is advisable to walk slowly. Follow the track south then east from the mountain station of the cable car. This track joins footpath 715 to the Velillscharte (*Scharte* means fissure) at 2,556m (8,384ft), which should take 45 minutes. The 715 is a good path which goes down the Velilltal to join a road before the village. Total time for walking is $2^1/_2$ hours.

Another interesting walk from Ischgl is across the Swiss border to the Heidelberger Hut (2,264m, 7,426ft). Drive up the Fimbertal to the guest house Bodenalpe (1,842m, 6,042ft) then walk up the good track. There are no border formalities. Time required is 4 hours and it is easy going. Once across the Swiss border the valley becomes the attractive Val Fenga surrounded by peaks almost 3,000m (9,840ft) high.

There are three more villages on the way down the valley, all picturesque and perched on terraces to catch the sun. Woods become denser and the road still follows the torrent of the river. A glimpse ahead to Wiesberg Castle marks the end of the valley. The castle is at one end of the famous Trisannabrücke a railway bridge of light and slender metal which adds great attraction to the view from its height of 82m (269ft) above the foaming river.

Now the route goes back to the west, along the Stanzertal to the Arlberg Pass. The first hamlet is **Strengen**, which lies in a ravine, and the next is **Flirsch**, which lies in pastureland. This variety is part of the charm of the route. Be sure to follow the signs for St Christoph am Arlberg, as the new main road takes the Arlberg Tunnel. **Pettneu** is a charming little village set safely back off the main road; a nearby church has a memorial to the men who died constructing the tunnel.

Wide meadows lie to the south of Pettneu with woods to the north. Behind the woods rise the massive limestone crags of the Lechtaler Alps, showing very pale in the bright sunshine. South are the snowy heights of the Hohe Riffler with the peaks glistening with snow.

**St Anton am Arlberg** is next, a name to lift the hearts of dedicated skiers. It is on a main railway route and the famous Arlberg Express stops here, so access is easy. Alpine skiing was devised and taught here as early as 1901, the method having been developed by an Austrian named Hannes Schneider. In 1926 he made a film *The Wonders of Skiing* which was a tremendous success. Arnold Lunn, the founder of the British Kandahar Ski Club, introduced slalom gates in 1922. In 1927 the two men met and their collaboration resulted in the first Arlberg-Kandahar Cup Race in St Anton in 1928.

The ski runs are mainly above the tree line but this does not mean there is nothing to do in summer. There are nearby woodland walks, fishing and mountain walks. A chair lift goes up, in two stages, to 2,333m (7,652ft) and a cable car goes up to the Valluga at 2,809m (9,213ft). There is a tourist information office in the town to check all the latest details.

For the energetic there are plenty of walks. The two-stage chair lift has its middle station at Gampen where there is a mountain restaurant and a signposted walk back down through the woods to the town. For a longer, more exciting walk take the chair lift to the top station, the Kapall House at 2,333m (7,652ft). Follow the path north from the hut then take the right fork. Follow the red marks on the rocky path. After $1^1/_4$ hour's walking the path reaches the Leutkircher Hut (2,252m 7,387ft), following national path 601. This is a high level path, part of the Lechtaler Hohenweg. Path 642 goes back to St Anton, the total time is $3^1/_4$ hours.

From St Anton continue the climb to the summit of the pass at 1,771m (5,808ft). **St Christoph am Arlberg** is just before the summit proper. A hospice was built here in 1386; unfortunately it burnt down in 1957 and the new building is the Hospice Hotel. Only part of the original chapel remains and is joined to the hotel. Visitors may peer into it through a special viewing window.

Buses cross the pass on the Bludenz to Landeck route and also run up the Flexenpath road to Lech. About 1km ($^1/_2$ mile) on the Vorarlberg side of the pass, take the right fork to the Flexenpass

*Near the top of the Hochtannberg Pass*

*Lech* (right) *is a fashionable winter sports resort*

⇐*The Silvretta Road climbing to the Bielerhöhe Pass, which joins the Montafon and Paznaun valleys*

and on to Lech. This is actually back in the Vorarlberg. From the first sharp bend there is a magnificent view, over the first tiny hamlet of Stuben just below, down the Klostertal with the peaks of the Rätikon Mountains in the distance. Climbing up towards the pass the road clings to the side of the mountain and required the building of almost three-quarters of a mile of galleries to protect the road from avalanches. This road is kept open all year round as over the pass is the tiny hamlet of Zürs.

The valley widens just before **Zürs** is reached. Most of the big hotels and the shops will be closed until November when the snow arrives and, with the snow, thousands of skiers. This treeless sunny valley boasts no less than eleven ski tows. One chair lift, in two stages, goes up to 2,702m (8,863ft). It is a paradise of alpine flowers in summer, while in winter there may be anything from 6 to 16ft (2 to 5m) of snow.

A gentle slope leads down from Zürs to Lech. Although it is argued that Zürs is more fashionable as a ski resort, **Lech** is a genuine, and very pretty, village at 1,447m (4,746ft). Lech has more facilities than Zürs. There are five cable cars, sixteen chair lifts, thirteen T-bar lifts, two ski schools, two ski kindergartens plus a toboggan run and a cross country ski trail. Also in winter there are walking trails, an ice skating rink and horse-drawn sleighs. The winter season is from the end of November to the end of April. It is possible to take a cable car from Lech to the Rufikopf (2,350m, 7,708ft), then to ski down to Zürs where there is a double chair lift to the Madlochjoch (2,438m, 7,997ft), from where it is possible to ski down the Stierloch to Zug and back to Lech.

Summer visitors will find over 240km (150 miles) of hiking trails, a heated outdoor swimming pool, a shooting range and river rafting. A lovely riverside walk from the southern end of the village. Take the road, then the footpath, to the south of the river. There is a heated swimming pool about 600m (1,968ft) along. The path leads along the beautiful upper Lech valley to **Zug** where there is a bridge over the river to the village. This is a low level riverside walk of a little under 2km (1 mile). For the more energetic, the path continues along the south side of the river for another 2km. A bridge takes a track over the river to the road. This road is a dead-end so there is little traffic other than holiday-makers visiting the upper reaches of the valley. Alternatively, take a horse drawn cart up to Zug and walk back down the river.

It is lovely, both in summer and winter! Lech has many shops but is expensive, reflecting the rich and the famous who come here to ski. It is also very picturesque, especially from the covered wooden bridge looking downstream towards the church.

The road to **Warth** is fairly level over its distance of about 6km (4 miles). It is a small village in a beautiful mountain setting. It is very pleasant to sit outside one of the *Gasthöfe* here in the midday sun which may be a coffee and *Apfelstrudel* (apple pie) an Austrian delicacy. Behind the village is the Beberkopf rising to a height of 2,599m (8,525ft). If you bear left here, the road rises to the Hochtannberg Pass. A new road beyond it greatly assists the descent to Au. Although the pass is quiet in summer, there are usually several policemen trying to sort order out of the chaos from the hundreds of cars trying to park here amid the snow. Here the road turns right towards Reutte and soon the River Lech is in view again. This stretch of road from Warth to Reutte, is an interesting touring road. It has made its name as a haven of peace. Quite away from the bustle of the main touring centres, it is an area where many will want to linger and although quieter, it has a great deal to offer. To the south tower the majestic Lechtaler Alps. To really get the feel of the Alps go up one of the side valleys to the mountain villages of Madau south of Bach, Gramais south of Häselgehr, Hinterhornbach via Vorderhornbach west of Stanzach, or Hamlos to the east.

The valley has numerous hotels, inns and pensions. It is possible just to relax, to stroll gently through the meadows, or to aim for the higher regions. For example, from the mountain village of **Madau** it is possible, on a good path, to climb up to the  Memminger Hut at 2,242m (7,354ft). Good mountain walkers can go beyond up to the three summits of the Zeekopf. The summits are a scramble and are all about 2,700m (8,856ft) in altitude. However, the valley does quickly loose the sun in mid-winter.

Down in the valley there is the 'High Green Footpath' from **Bach** to **Häselgehr**. There are at least three swimming pools in the area and facilities for many other sports including climbing.

The mighty Alps dominate the scenery with the Allgäuer Alps to the north-west. However, the eye is constantly drawn back to the river. Though this powerful giant may be in gentle mood in the summer season, large areas of flood wash demonstrate the rise of water in the spring thaw. When all the side streams are in spate the power and noise of the main river is awesome.

In the pretty village of **Elbigenalp** there is a small professional wood carving school where the Tyrolean tradition of wood carving is maintained. Alongside the main church, which is seventeenth-century and stands in fields slightly apart from the village, is the fifteenth-century Chapel of St Martin. The crypt once served as a charnel house and there are painted panels in the chapel representing the *Dance of the Dead*.

At **Weissenbach** there is an interesting side valley, the Tannheimer, on road 199, and a lakeside campsite at the Haldensee. The valley is claimed to be one of the most beautiful in Europe.

The road then leads on to **Reutte** which is the administrative and tourist capital of the Ausserfern. The Ausserfern means 'beyond the Fern', the Fern in this case being the Fernpass, which cuts off the area from the main Inn valley. Reutte is a pleasant town and a convenient centre for a few days' exploration. In keeping with the area there are some colourfully painted houses and an interesting small museum.

*Warth in the Lechtal*

From Reutte take the road toward Füssen to visit the **Lech Falls**  where the mighty river tumbles down onto the Bavarian plain. There is a small layby and a viewing platform. Then it is possible to continue to Schwangau and to visit the two castles described at the start of the chapter.

A minor road goes from Reutte to Plansee where there are campsites. It is also possible to drive along the 314 road to **Heiterwang,** which is bypassed by the main road, and where there is another campsite on the Heiterwang See. The two lakes are joined by a narrow canal.

An easy day's walk is available from any point round both  lakes. Fascinating views unfold as the walker proceeds. It is probably better to start from Heiterwang and walk the eastern bank of both lakes. This is because from the head of Plansee a motorboat service operates to the centre point and then back to Hotel Fischer Am See at the Heiterwang end. Anyone becoming tired could take a ride part of the way back. Plansee is the larger of the two lakes, nearly 6km (4 miles) long.

Just outside Reutte is a mountain railway taking visitors to a  height of almost 2,000m (6,560ft) where there is a fascinating alpine flower garden and the 'Alpine Rose Path' for a pleasant  stroll. Or there is a cable car to the Hofener Alm which opens up a delightful network of paths with fantastic mountain views. Beyond Heiterwang the road undulates before gently descending to Lermoos.

## *Additional Information*

### *Places of Interest*

**Reutte**
*Alpine Gardens*
Reached via the Reutte cable car, the Reuttener Bergbahn, south-west of Reutte near Hofen.
☎ (4567) 22420

**Schwangau** (Germany)
*Schloss Neuschwanstein* and *Schloss Hohenschwangau*
Open: April to end September daily 8.30am-5.30pm; October to end March daily 10am-4pm.

**St Anton am Arlberg**
*Ski and Folk Museum*
Open: all day in summer.

## Tourist Information Offices

**Bach**
A-6653
☎ (5634) 6778

**Elbigenalp**
A-6652
☎ (5634) 6270

**Flirsch**
A-6572
☎ (5447) 5564

**Galtür**
A-6563
☎ (5443) 204, 414

**Gargellen**
A-6787
☎ (5557) 6303

**Gaschurn**
A-6793
☎ (5558) 8201

**Häselgehr**
A-6651
☎ (5634) 6600

**Heiterwang**
A-6611
☎ (5674) 5103

**Ischgl**
A-6561
☎ (5444) 5266, 5314

**Lech**
A-6764
☎ (5583) 2161-0

**Partenen**
A-6794
☎ (5558) 8315

**Pettneu**
A-6574
☎ (5448) 221

**Reutte**
A-6600
☎ (5672) 2336, 2041

**St Anton / St Christoph am Arlberg**
A-6580
☎ (5446) 22690

**St Gallenkirch / Gortipohl**
A-6791
☎ (5557) 6600

**Schruns**
A-6780
☎ (5556) 2166, 2167

**Strengen**
A-6571
☎ (5447) 5837

**Stuben**
A-6762
☎ (5582) 761

**Tschagguns**
A-6774
☎ (5567) 2457

**Warth**
A-6767
☎ (5583) 3515

**Weissenbach / Lech**
A-6671
☎ (5678) 5303

**Zürs**
A-6763
☎ (5583) 2245

# 3
# EHRWALD, THE UPPER INN
# & THE SOUTHERN VALLEYS

The main 314 road goes from Reutte to Imst and is joined by the 187 to Lermoos. This route comes in from the very pictur-esque German town of Garmisch-Partenkirchen.

Trains run regularly from Reutte along the valley to Lermoos and Ehrwald. The line comes in from Füssen in Germany and returns to Germany at Garmishch-Partenkirchen. To get from here to Innsbruck by train one first starts off in the wrong direction, north to Garmisch then via Mittenwald and back into Austria at Scharnitz. Post buses run from Reutte to Innsbruck via Lermoos and Ehrwald.

This area is a popular winter and summer resort. **Ehrwald** is 'on the sunny side of the Zugspitze', to quote the town's own claim. It is certainly well equipped, as well as any other in the area. There is a heated indoor swimming pool with sun terrace and, right next door, a sports hall. To the west of the town, across the footbridge near the tennis courts, are larch woods and a most lovely walk along gentle gradients.

At the other end of the town is the road up to Obermoos. A footpath goes up through the woods, as does the Zugspitze cable car, a most impressive ride. If you are in luck you may spot chamois below. Higher up look out for walkers scrambling up the path from the Wiener-Neustadter Hut. This is a wonderful walk for very experienced hill walkers/scramblers involving about 1,800m (5,900ft) of ascent and taking about 6 hours from Ehrwald. It is an unforgettable experience, if the weather is fair, to climb up and spend the night at the Münchener Haus (an alpine hut at the summit), to watch the sunset and then get up

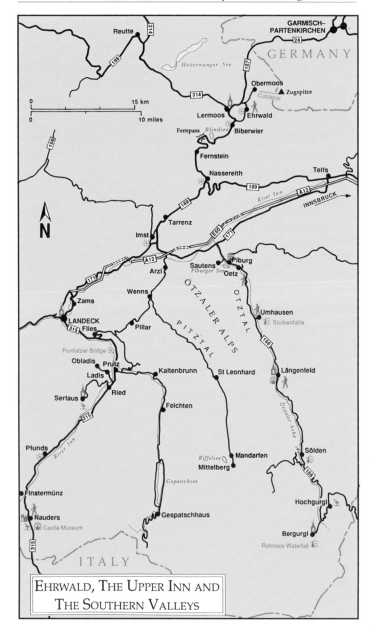

EHRWALD, THE UPPER INN AND
THE SOUTHERN VALLEYS

*Taking a well-earned rest at the Coburger Hut in the mountains near Ehrwald*

*The Moos and Lermoos with the Sonnenspitze*

early to watch the sunrise. Follow this by the walk back to Ehrwald via the Knorr Hut and the Gatterl. The view from the top of the Zugspitze is breathtaking. To the south-east are the High Tauern and the Zillertal Alps. Due south are the Otztaler Alps with the Silvretta more westerly. North of the Silvretta are the Lechtaler Alps. This forms a breathtaking panorama on a clear day. There is a border post on the summit and passports may be checked. The westerly summit of the Zugspitze is in Austria but the highest point, 2,962m (9,715ft) is in Germany. A scramble with ropes and steps permits access to the summit with its cross.

Many summits have crosses on them, many of which were erected privately by ordinary citizens as a personal token of gratitude. An early start is recommended as in high season the tops often get crowded. On the Austrian side there is a restaurant and enclosed viewing area as well as the outside platform. Across the German border there is the previously mentioned Münchener Haus, a restaurant, a cable car down to Eibsee in Germany, and also a cable car down to Schneeferner Haus near the snowfields where there is good skiing until very late in the year. The Schneeferner Haus is the terminus for a railway up from Garmisch-Partenkirchen. Many people use the terraces for sunbathing but at this altitude great care must be taken. The air is thinner but cooler so tender skin will burn quickly.

Another splendid walk here for every experienced walkers is as follows. Go down to the lowest level of the Schneeferner Haus, out onto the terrace and down the steps onto the snow. Follow the snowfield down, following a line of posts to the Knorr Hut which may be reached in $1^1/_2$ hours. From the hut go right, along level ground at first, to Gatterl, a narrow break in the ridge forming the border (no formalities) and follow the path right down a narrow chimney with a fixed rope. Go along to another ridge. Go right again, looking out for chamois and marmots. At the next ridge the path is obvious: follow it down to the Hochfelder Alm (refreshments) and the Ehrwalder Alm. You may be lucky enough to catch the last cable car down the valley at 5pm if the start is early enough. Total walking time is 7 hours. There is some rough going — nothing a good hill walker would not enjoy — with fantastic scenery.

For the less ambitious, a trip up the Ehrwald Alm cable car opens up the higher level meadows for a walk without the effort of the climb. A gentle stroll up to the Pest Kepelle (Plague Chapel) is a delight in spring or early summer when the flowers are at their best. At a time when the Black Death was rampant in Europe, the villagers were about to set off on a pilgrimage when the local militia from the next valley met them and prevented them from going on. The plague did not reach the valley and later the chapel was erected in commemoration by grateful villagers. There is a variety of entertainment in the town. A Tyrolean evening may be enjoyed in one of the local hotels and a host of entertainment is put on by various establishments.

Moos means moss and the central flat area shows signs of once being peat, but is now well drained grassland criss-crossed with paths which make pleasant level walking. Across the Moos is **Lermoos**, another pleasant resort where the church is well worth a visit. A chair lift goes up in two stages to the Grübigstein (2,040m, 6,691ft), with the possibility of walking down, or at least over the meadows of the lower half.

**Biberwier** takes up the remaining space in the valley, a pleasant little village now bypassed by the main road. Biberwier's claim to fame is a visible section of the old Roman road, the *Via Claudia Augusta*, named after Emperor Claudius who rebuilt the road in AD46. Just above the village, off the Fernpass road, there is a *Rodelbahn* or dry bobsleigh run in the summer. A chair lift whisks passengers up to descend what looks like half a pipe, on a small go-cart-type contraption. No steering is necessary, the only control being a fast-slow device like a joystick.

The ascent of the Fernpass starts at Biberwier. Take time to stop at the lakes on the way up. Weisensee and Mittersee are splendidly set in woodland with grassy banks and paths round them. The largest lake, the Blindsee, is the highest. Delightfully set in a fold of the hills it has a deep green tint which is fully complemented by the forest and the limestone crags above. Road access has made this a popular swimming spot and whole families gather to enjoy a day at the lakeside once the summer sun has warmed the water.

Beyond the lake the summit of the Fernpass is soon reached; at only 1,210m (3,969ft) it is quite gentle in alpine terms. There is a large car park just before the summit and from the terrace of the restaurant there is probably the best view back to the Wetterstein group and the peak of the Sonnenspitze to the north.

Below the summit on the south side **Fernstein** is soon reached. A castle sits above the road guarding the bridge, while below is the lovely Fernsteinsee. The wooded banks of this deep set lake complement the green waters and the tree filled island. Boating and swimming are available and there is a nearby campsite.

❋ **Nassereith** is the next village, where the main square is a stopping place for the Innsbruck to Reutte post bus service. Behind the square is the old part of the village with some nice old houses and a tiny lake. The village is well known for its carnival procession which is held every 5 years. These February carnivals are held in turn by Nassereith, Imst and Telfs to drive out the bad spirits of winter and to prepare for the return of spring. It has its origins in old Pagan customs and the costumed figures wear grotesque masks. When not in use these are kept in Innsbruck at the Tiroler Volkskunstmuseum or Tyrol Museum of Popular Art. There is a campsite near the village.

❋ **Imst**, a few miles beyond Tarrenz, is a thriving market town-

*Looking towards the Zugspitze*
*from a path on the Grubigstein above Lermoos* ⇒

*The Blindsee — one of the many lakes in the Tyrol suitable for bathing*

ship and is an excellent centre for exploration of the surrounding area. The town lies back from the River Inn and the railway, and it has two adjacent campsites.

The Upper Town, or Oberstadt, which nestles round the old parish church is most attractive. Destroyed by fire in 1822, it was rebuilt using the original Gothic doorways. Outside there is a giant statue of St Christopher, while pretty fountains and rounded window grilles make a most attractive sight.

Among the figures of the carnival processions are those of bird sellers. During the seventeenth century canary breeders from Imst traded as far afield as Madrid and St Petersburg. They even had their own depot in London. Trade began to fall off as competition grew from the popular singing birds of the Harz district. Then in the disastrous fire of 1822 many houses were destroyed, including those of the canary breeders, and the trade came to an end.

From Imst go south-west on road 171. The River Inn soon comes into view and this is crossed to reach the village of **Schönwies** then re-crossed soon after leaving. There is a campsite at Schönwies.

Soon the valley narrows and becomes more wooded. The tiny village of **Zamserberg** nestles in the woods below the ruins of Kronburg, a medieval castle.

Within a few kilometres **Zams** is reached, from the bridge of which there is a magnificent view of the ruins of Schrofenstein to the south-west. From here it is another 4km (2 miles) to Landeck.

**Landeck** is a small industrial town and an important centre, standing as it does at the junction of the Inn valley and the Arlberg road. The massive feudal castle dates from the thirteenth century. This, and the other strong points perched like eagles' nests round about, silently testify to the ancient strategic importance of the valley junction.

Though Landeck lacks the charm of Imst it still enjoys popularity as a tourist town. It is a useful centre from which to explore the nearby Oberinntal and Kaunertal and is the main centre and shopping town for the area. The parish church, standing on a terrace below the castle, is well worth a visit. It is a carefully planned Gothic building and the fifteenth-century network vaulting is worth inspecting, as is the centre piece of the altar. Dating from the sixteenth century the work represents the *Ado-*

*ration of the Magi*; the side panels are of later date.

Nearby are Stanz, Tabadill, Fliess and Grins, all good examples of pretty Tyrolean villages. **Grins** was the favourite spa of Margarete, the Margravin of the Tyrol. Being a widow, and having lost her son, she bequethed her country to the Habsburgs in January 1363; a few months later she abdicated and spent the rest of her life in Vienna.

From Landeck take the 315 road following the river to the higher reaches of the Inntal. Near the border, just beyond Pfunds, the road divides, the 315 going over the Reschenpass into Italy while another branch, now the 184, goes into Switzerland.

The valley is a paradise for walkers of all standards or, indeed, for anyone wanting a healthy active holiday. This is the area where it is claimed that the sun shines longer and more brightly than anywhere else.

Heading upstream the Engadine valley in Switzerland can soon be reached via a narrow cleft between mountains. It is possible to cross into Switzerland then back to Austria a little further along at Martina. A short steep climb on a secondary road brings one back to Nauders.

A beautiful short walk starts from the highest point of this road, the Norberthöhe. Go west from the Norberthöhe and in 20 minutes the Schopfwarte (1,438m, 4,717ft) is reached. This fortification was built before World War I and later enlarged. There is a most splendid view from here to the lower Engadine and the surrounding mountains. A further five minutes and another spectacular view is reached, this time of the Inn gorge deep below. Follow the path, marked 2, meandering in a northerly direction before swinging round the Selleskopfe eventually to return to the starting point. There is another spectacular view, down to the Finstermünz gorge, on the way round. The whole walk is easy going and should be completed in 2 hours.

**Nauders** lies in a basin where crops are grown despite the altitude of nearly 1,400m (4,600ft). It is mainly a winter sport resort. The castle began life as an administrative centre for the Upper Inn valley but during the Swiss Wars of Independence gained in strategic importance. However, the real strategic spot on this route is at **Finstermünz**, or old Finstermünz to be precise. The old road crossed the river at the Innbrucke and a tower was built to straddle the road. This was backed up by a second tower and natural caves gave more space. Successive enlargements have left nothing earlier than fifteenth century.

From Hochfinstermünz the road clings to the eastern bank on the cliffs. There is a stopping place on this corniche overlooking the gorge and the tributary gorge leading up to the Samnaun valley in Switzerland. The main valley is reached at the Kajetanbrucke from where it is 2km (1 mile) downstream to **Pfunds**. Here there are really two villages — Pfunds Stuben and Pfunds Dorf, divided by the river. In the village there are a number of fine old inns and houses which are typical of the area. Express horse-drawn coaches used to run this way to Meron in Italy and to Switzerland. Pfunds was one of the post stations and in a village of this size there would have been anything up to fifty horses.

Fourteen kilometres (9 miles) down the valley from Pfunds is **Ried** from where there is a side turning to the left up to the interesting villages of **Ladis**, with its little white bell tower and nearby ruins of Laudeck, and to **Serfaus**. The latter is an impor-

*Landeck*

tant winter sports centre with many ski lifts and, more important to the summer visitor, a cable car going up to a height of 2,000m (6,560ft). Ladis, in particular, is well worth a visit to see the old houses with outside staircases and separate baking ovens. Serfaus has a fourteenth-century church and a Baroque church, and some pretty painted houses.

**Fendels**, by Prutz, is a typical small Tyrolean village in an area of meadows with woods and a background of mountains. At **Prutz** a tributary comes in to join the Inn, and a view opens up easterly of the Kaunergrat with its jagged skyline.

From the head of the deep-cut Kaunertal there is a walk along the lake shore to a mountain hut. The road is closed to traffic at the Gepatsch (1,767m, 5,796ft) and it is a pleasant walk along the lake with splendid mountain views. Allow 3 hours for the round trip, which is easy going.The Kauntertal also has summer skiing on Gepatsch glacier, high above the valley floor. A road runs up to the ski lodge and the skiing is between 2,750m (9,020ft) and 3,160m (10,365ft). This peaceful valley has variety from the glaciers of the mountain tops to the sunbathing on the lawn outside the sports centre, with its indoor pool and bowling alleys.

The Pontlatzer Bridge and a memorial lies 4km (2 miles) downstream from Prutz. In 1342 the earliest European democratic constitution was granted to the Tyrol by Meinhard II. All classes were guaranteed their rights and serfdom was unknown. In 1511 a law was passed granting all Tyroleans the right to bear arms. No-one of any class could be called to serve elsewhere but all had to be ready at all times to defend the Tyrol. In 1703 the Bavarians and the French attacked. Such was the surprise that the authorities in Innsbruck surrendered, but the inhabitants of the South Tyrol and the Inn valley forced the invaders to withdraw with heavy losses on the Brenner, at Rattenberg, and here at the Pontlatz Bridge. The memorial also commemorates the defeat in 1809 of a French force marching on Finstermunz.

This historic right and duty of the Tyrolean to bear arms is reflected in the area today. Most villages have a rifle brigade, and a feature of many of them is an open evening when visitors are invited to shoot.

A little further downstream a minor road goes right to **Flies** and **Piller**. These two small typical villages are on route to Wenns and the Piztal and make a pleasant quiet drive away from the tourist beat. Flies has a heated swimming pool and facilities for tennis and fishing.

The Piztal begins at Imst and ends abruptly after about 30km (19 miles) at Mittelberg and the steely blue shimmering ice wall of a glacier. The several villages along the length of the valley cater for mountain holidays. There are frequent guided walks in the valley and qualified guides are available to accompany rock and ice climbing parties.

From the village of **Mandarfen** at 1,682m (5,517ft) there is a chair lift up to a height of 2,298m (7,537ft). This is the Riffelsee chair lift, or *Sesselbahn*. From the top of the chair lift it is an easy climb, of about 15 minutes, to the summit of the Mutten Kogel (2,346m, 7,695ft), from where there is a splendid view of the lake and surrounding mountains. Near the end of the lake lies the Riffelsee hut with good lake views. The Riffelsee is the largest natural lake in the Ötzaler Alps.

Path 926 returns to the valley, twisting and turning down to the Taschachalm. From the *Alm* a road returns to Mandarfen in 1$\frac{1}{2}$km (1 mile). Total time required is 1$\frac{1}{2}$ hours and the going is easy.

To get to the next valley one must go down to the main Inn valley again via Arzl. Another major tributory, the Ötztaler Ache, joins the Inn 6km (4 miles) downstream from here. The Ötztaler will be remembered for its thundering river and for the shining glaciers. It is a deep valley 36km (22 miles) long with ravines separated by more open flatter basins. In 1969 the Timmelsjoch road was completed and the valley ceased to be a dead end. There is now a route, albeit in summer only, south into Italy.

**Obergurgl** stands in a combe at the head of the valley and is the highest village in Austria with a church. In the small square there is a magnificent statue of an old fashioned mountain guide with outstretched hand pointing to the mountains. A chair lift goes in two stages to the Hohe Mut at 2,670m (8,758ft) where there is a grassy knoll with a mountain restaurant and fantastic views. It is said that twenty-one glaciers can be seen from here. There are certainly snow capped peaks on every side and magnificent waterfalls in the gorges just above the village.

An easy walk to the Rotmoos Waterfall starts from the end of the village road. Follow path 922 which goes to the Schönwieshütte. Over the Gaisberg Bridge turn right onto path 9 to the Rotmoos stream. The stream is magnificent as it hurtles down the ravine. The path back follows path 7 through the beautiful Zirbenwald. The time for the walk should be about 2 hours, easy going on good paths.

At the nearby village of **Hochgurgl** (2,150m, 7,052ft) there is a heated indoor pool and a chair lift in three stages to a height of over 3,000m (10,000ft) where skiing is available all year round.

Down the valley is **Sölden**, a tourist village popular in both winter and summer. Here there is a cable car which has a spectacular start directly over the main road. It goes up to a height of 3,058m (10,030ft) to the Geislacherkogel where there are breathtaking views of the entire range of the Örztal Alps.

Sölden is also the point of departure for one of the highest roads in the Alps, which at its highest point is 2,822m (9,256ft). This gives access to winter and summer skiing. There is a toll charge for use of the road. Hochsölden is the tourist annexe of the old village: a chair lift operates between the two, joining the higher collection of hotels with the village itself.

The largest village in the valley is **Längenfeld**. Nestling in an angle of the valley, the village is really divided into two separate halves by the Fischbach which hurls itself down a side valley from the south-east. There are well prepared walks in the larch woods near the village. On the west side of the valley is a seventeenth-century plague chapel. The scenery is hard with peaks which seem to close in all round. Längenfeld was the birthplace of Franz Senn, the founder of the Austrian Alpine Club. There is a small local museum here.

Even at this height crops are grown. Indeed they are grown even higher up the valley, the reason being that the upper end of the Ötztal has a channel between the peaks through which a current of warm southerly air finds its way. This current keeps the valleys warm and dry and allows even barley, for example, to be grown at a height of 1,700m (5,576ft).

While Längenfeld is the largest village in the valley, **Um-hausen** is the oldest. A large inn, the Gasthaus Krone, is typical of the district. Customers of the inn may see a room still furnished in seventeenth-century style. From the tourist office a signposted track leads to the Stuibenfalle, a picturesque cascade where the torrent tumbles down the rocky ravine. At a chalet-restaurant cross the stream and walk up the left bank. About 2 hours are required for the walk.

**Oetz** (or Ötz) is the last village on the return trip down the valley. The large village church is built on a level spot on the sunny slope.

The warm southerly air current, or Föhn, which blows down the valley can transform life and allows peach and apricot orchards to thrive in the Oetz basin. On the other hand, its ill effects are widely acknowledged: examinations may be suspended in schools, Föhn headaches are infamous, at its worst it can be used as extenuating circumstances in criminal trials.

✳ Near Oetz is the hamlet of **Piburg** with the Piburger See at 915m (3,001ft). This jewel of a lake has a fascinating history. In 1282 it was given to Stams Monastery which had recently been founded. Until 1500 meat was forbidden to the monks so the fish yield of the lake was important. The monks' rights to the lake were reaffirmed in 1339 by Duke Johann and again in 1616 by Archduke Max. For 600 years the lake remained as a holding of the monastery. The tenants of nearby Piburg were forbidden to fish. A story is told that in the nineteenth century bathers caused such frequent annoyance to the monks that the lake was sold.

It was sometime around the end of the century when the first bathing hut was built for the convenience of hotel guests from Oetz. In 1929 the lake and surrounds were declared a nature conservation area. The first freshwater studies were carried out in 1931, but today these are confined to a bay at the northern end so they do not intrude upon the landscape. The Piburger See remains one of the few completely natural unspoilt lakes anywhere in Europe despite its use as an amenity. This use has been very carefully controlled and in 1982, when a new bathing establishment was added, it was built on concrete pillars and anchored to the bank in order to avoid felling trees.

🚶 There is a parking area near the beginning of Piburg and there are lakeside walks in magnificent unspoilt scenery. The lake temperature can get as high as 24°C (75°F) in summer, making it quite comfortable and one of the warmest lakes in the Tyrol.

Below Oetz the main road along the Inn valley is reached once more. Turn eastwards along the 171 towards Innsbruck.

# Additional Information

## Places of Interest

**Landeck**
*Castle Museum*
Open: May to September 10am-5pm.

**Nauders**
*Fortress and Museum*
Open: mid-May to mid-October. Guided tours of the castle Sunday 10am-5pm; tours of museum on Wednesday, Saturday and Sunday at 2pm.

## Tourist Information Centres

**Biberwier**
A-6633
☎ (5673) 2922

**Ehrwald**
A-6632
☎ (5673) 2395

**Flies**
A-6521
☎ (5449) 5224

**Grins**
A-6591
☎ (5442) 3827

**Imst**
A-6460
☎ (5412) 2419

**Ladis**
A-6531
☎ (5472) 6601

**Landeck**
A-6500
☎ (5442) 2344

**Längenfeld**
A-6444
☎ (5253) 5207

**Lermoos**
A-6631
☎ (5673) 2401

**Nassereith**
A-6465
☎ (5265) 5253

**Nauders**
A-6543
☎ (5473) 220

**Obergurgl / Hochgurgl**
A-6456
☎ (5256) 258, 353

**Oetz**
A-6433
☎ (5252) 6669

**Pfunds / Oberinntal**
A-6542
☎ (5474) 5229

**Prutz / Faggen / Fendels**
A-6522
☎ (5472) 6267

**Ried / Oberinntal**
A-6531
☎ (5472) 6421

**Schönwies**
A-6491
☎ (5418) 5238

**Serfaus**
A-6534
☎ (5476) 6239

**Sölden / Hochsölden**
A-6450
☎ (5254) 2212-0

**Umhausen**
A-6441
☎ (5255) 5209

**Zams**
A-6511
☎ (5442) 3395

# 4
# *AROUND INNSBRUCK*

The first place of any significance on the road to Innsbruck is **Stams** where the monastery is very well worth a visit. It was founded by Elizabeth of Bavaria to the memory of her son, Conradin Hohenstaufen, beheaded in Naples on the order of Charles of Anjou in 1268. Unfortunately, she did not live to see its consecration. The monastery rapidly gained in influence and, until 1600, all sovereign princes of the Tyrol were buried there.

This majestic building was made more conspicuous in the seventeenth century by the addition of two towers. There is room to park in the esplanade near the fourteenth-century village church and the entrance is through the abbey gateway to the porter's lodge. Altered many times, the present Baroque style is the result of the last rebuilding in the eighteenth century. The showpiece of the abbey church is the high altar with its representation of the Tree of Life. The branches are formed by eighty-four carved figures of saints surrounding the Virgin. On either side Adam and Eve represent life's beginning, while, at the top, Christ on the cross represents the mystery of the supernatural.

The Hall of Princes is reached by a staircase with a fine wrought iron balustrade going up from the porter's lodge. In the Hall of State paintings depict many episodes in the life of St Bernard. A guided tour and an English language brochure are available.

**Telfs**, only 7km (4 miles) from Stams, is a typical market town. It was the limit of navigation on the Inn and even then could only be used by smaller boats. Here everything had to be unloaded for transporting overland up the Fernpass or up to the Arlberg or Engadine.

The masked dances and carnivals of Telfs are prehistoric in origin. They will probably never die although perhaps the reason for them has altered. The Tyrolean love of pageant and play-acting will ensure their survival even if the tourist industry does not.

From Telfs there is a minor road towards Mösern and Seefeld in Tyrol. The splendid site of the village of **Mösern** makes an ideal place to stop. On the way up to the village there are splendid retrospective views, towards the north-west, of the Mieminger Mountains. On a grassy spur below the church is the Gashof Inntal from where there is a view of the River Inn, upstream in the Telfs furrow, before it disappears from view in a tangle of peaks, some covered with snow.

**Seefeld im Tyrol** is 5km (3 miles) away. It is an elegant place with a high reputation as a ski resort due to the fact that the Winter Olympics were twice held here. Both a winter and summer resort, it is one of the few places to boast a full size golf course. Facilities for riding are nearby and there is a casino. The sports centre has indoor and outdoor pools while there are twelve outdoor and four indoor tennis courts. Rowing, fishing, bowling and mini golf are all available and many of the hotels have their own pools and saunas.

The parish church is worth visiting. A Gothic building dating from the fifteenth century, it has interesting murals of the same date which have been restored. On the outskirts of the town is the Seekirchl, or lake chapel, standing beside a meadow which was once a small lake.

A minor road leaves Seefeld towards Leutasch, leading through a wooded landscape towards the charming unspoilt Leutasch valley. **Leutasch** itself is an attractive jumble of hamlets in a flat and broad valley. The covered heated swimming pool has a café/restaurant and a large outside sunbathing lawn. A climbing school, a riding school and two chair lifts complete the facilities. One chair lift to the south ascends to a height of 1,600m (5,248ft) from the hamlet of Moos to the Moos Alm on the eastern end of the ridge of the Hohe Munde, 2,592m (8,502ft) high. A good path climbs from the *Alm* to the summit.

The valley lies at the east foot of the Wetterstein Mountains, with the Karwendel range to the east and Mieminger range to the south-west. To return, drive north-east towards Mittenwald in

Germany, where border checks are minimal, but on the outskirts of the town turn back south to recross the border to Scharnitz.

The drive towards Mittenwald with the roofed roadside crosses, and houses with stones on their roofs to anchor them in winter gales, enables one to enjoy the primitive air of a high alpine valley.

**Scharnitz** is a pleasant border village with bus and rail links. It is mostly passed by people rushing south to Innsbruck or over the Brenner Pass to Italy. However it is a convenient place from which to explore the Isar valley or the Karwendel Mountains.

There are easy footpaths each side of the Karwendel range. East of the village, crossing the railway, the Pürzlweg climbs steeply to the Pürzl Kapelle, then follows the Karwendel valley, which is surprisingly level, to the Larchetalm on a good forest road. The Larchetalm is privately owned but higher up the valley is the Karwendelhaus. This is an alpine hut clinging to a rocky perch almost at the saddle before the descent to the Johannestal. It is a good walk — 2 hours to the Larchetalm, a further 2 to the

*Stams monastery*

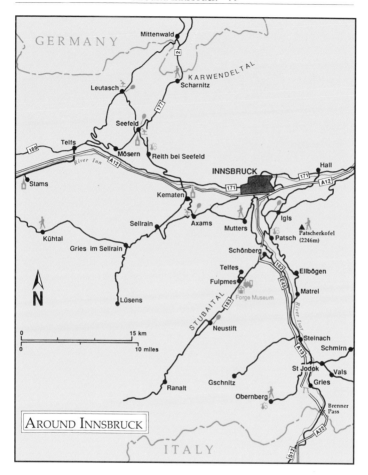

AROUND INNSBRUCK

Karwendelhaus, then the return walk. The valley is beautiful and entirely unspoilt; it is closed to traffic except for forestry, farmers and Larchetalm and Karwendelhaus vehicles. There are towering mountains on either side but with pleasant green meadows and woods on the lower slopes. The Karwendel Bach tumbles gaily down to be joined by side streams at many places.

There is a second walk which follows the River Isar upstream. On a small road at first, the road is closed to traffic just before the

Scharnitzer Alm is reached and it continues to follow the river. A little over a kilometre beyond the Wiesenhof, take a right fork which soon crosses the river. The next right fork leads to a path by which one can return on the south bank.

The next village is **Reith bei Seefeld** where the village church, in its charming setting, is worth a visit. Reith is at 1,130m (3,706ft) and from here the road plunges down into the Inn valley, passing the hamlet of Leithen. The well known slope down to the valley is called the Zirler Berg and there is a descent of 500m (1,640ft) in just over 4km (2 miles). At one time, so it is said, spectators used to collect near the hairpin bends to watch for accidents. Before improvements the road was as steep as 1 in 4, but is now 1 in 7 with only one hairpin bend. There is a car park and café and a splendid viewpoint over the Rosskögel to the Kalkkögel ridge to the south.

The Inn valley carries the motorway and the main road to Innsbruck but due south is another of the charming unspoilt valleys so typical of the Tyrol, the Sellrain. This is easily reached from Innsbruck by bus and is very popular with the locals as a winter sports area. In summer the valley villages are starting points for tours of the Stubai glaciers.

**Kühtai** stands at the head of the valley at 1,966m (6,448ft) on a plateau with the renowned hunting lodge of Maxmilian I, now converted to a hotel. Beyond the pass, 2,017m (6,616ft) high, the road goes down to Oetz (see Chapter 3).

There is a minor road to the south just beyond the pass. A little way down this road there is a footpath which forks to the left. It soon forks right to the Finstertaler Speicher, one of the larger lakes formed by a dam. Path 146 starts from the Hotelsiedlung Kühtai and is easy going, taking about $1^3/_4$ hours. There are splendid views and the many small lakes in the area ornament the landscape like jewels.

Coming back down the valley the villages of **St Sigmund**, and **Gries im Sellrain** may be found. Here a side valley south to the hamlets of **Praxmar** and **Lüsens** provides an ideal place to get away from the crowds and to enjoy the real Tyrol. The next village is **Sellrain** and, at the bottom of the valley, **Kematen**.

On emerging from the Sellrain valley there is a right turn on a minor road to Völs. There is a further right turn to Götzens through the village to Axams then up to Axamer-Lizum, 1,564m

(5,130ft). This was the site of the 1964 Winter Olympics and has a funicular, the Olympia Standseibahn, which carry passengers to the mountain station restaurant at 2,340m (7,675ft). A little downhill, to the Hoadl Sattel (2,264m, 7,426ft), leads to a grassy plateau which is rich in all kinds of alpine flowers. The paths are good and safe for a gentle stroll in the most beautiful mountain scenery.

**Axams** is a splendid old village with modern facilities for tourists. The swimming pool is delightful. There is a walking programme and facilities for cycle hire, with a cycle track laid out through the meadows. There are the usual musical events, band concerts, Tyrolean evenings and church concerts, while tennis, minigolf and bowling add to the attractions of this lovely centre which is only 9km (6 miles) from Innsbruck.

Nearby **Mutters**, which lies on moderately level ground, is a farming village which has kept its country air despite catering for tourists. It has a four-person cable car to the Mutter Alm, a twenty-minute ride to a splendid walking area. Near the village is a heated open-air pool (or pools as there are four if the paddling pools are included). These are surrounded by grassy banks for sunbathing while nearby are tennis courts. Scattered about the area are a number of camp sites.

Leaving Mutters, the road soon joins the main road 182. Innsbruck is only 2 or 3km away to the north. The Wipptal is south with its side valleys. The main valley carries the motorway over the Brenner Pass and has been a favourite route since the very earliest recorded history. It is the shortest route from Germany to Italy and was maintained and kept open, even in winter (which was no mean feat) by the Romans. The Wipptal is spanned by the famous Europabrucke.

There are four side valleys, the most famous of which is the Stubaital which offers splendid opportunities for mountain climbing. As an excellent excursion from Innsbruck there is the narrow gauge Stubai Valley Railway which trundles from village to village through glorious scenery to terminate at Fulpmes. Post buses run at frequent intervals from Innsbruck to Ranalt.

The road continues past Ranalt to **Mutterberg Alm** where the cable cars start for the glacier. The journey is in two parts with a break at the Dresdener Hut at 2,308m (7,570ft) before the next stage which goes up to 2,900m (9,512ft). Here there is all-year

skiing, walking on good safe paths, and, for the skiers, a double chair lift and seven tow lifts. Unless one intends to ski there is little point in using the top section of the cable car, instead take a stroll from the Dresdener Hut. There are paths to the Trögler (2,901m, 9,515ft) to the east or to the Egesengrat (2,631m, 8,630ft), west then north-east.

Ranalt is more or less a collection of farms at the foot of glaciers, while Volderau and Milders are hamlets offering peaceful stopping places in this delightful setting.

**Neustift** is another of those delightful villages that has everything to offer the visitor. Sixty kilometres (37 miles) of pathways are looked after by the local council who ensure that they are tidy, safe and secure, and with adequate signposting. There are two

⇐ *The beautiful and quiet Leutasch valley*

*The village of Mutters*

heated swimming pools, indoor and outdoor; the outdoor pool has a sunbathing lawn. Tennis can be played at nine outdoor and two indoor courts, and there is fishing and riding, together with the usual evening entertainments.

**Fulpmes**, terminus of the delightful little narrow gauge railway, is situated in broad green meadows below the forested approaches to the higher peaks. It has a variety of shops and restaurants, a tennis hall with a sliding roof which can be opened in warm weather, and a heated pool, and four campsites nearby.

The nearby hamlet of **Telfes** is one of those places which the discerning visitor will love. It is a genuine working community, with a farm in the main street, yet with comfortable and welcoming hotels. It sits on a plateau on the southern side of the valley, where it catches plenty of sunshine, and with far-reaching views towards the wooded slopes of the mountains. The surrounding meadows are carpeted with alpine flowers before they are cut with the hay in late June.

Just outside the village is a small bird park constructed to house a most interesting collection of birds of prey. The owner is happy to speak with visitors concerning his birds which may also be seen in action at certain times of the day when flown for exercise.

**Schönberg** stands at the junction of the main valley and the Stubai valley. The Wipptal is not one of the most beautiful valleys in the Tyrol but it is popular with the Austrians as a winter and summer resort. Up the valley, the first stop is **Matrei**, rebuilt in typical Tyrolean style after being almost completely destroyed during World War II. The houses blend well with the surroundings, many with attractive murals on the outside walls.

The next village is **Steinach**, where there is a lake and a swimming pool. Here also is a road branching off into the Gschnitztal, a short romantic valley with two hamlets, Trims and Gschnitz. Beyond Steinach the road climbs to **Gries**, which is not far from the head of the pass. Nearby there is a reminder that this was once a military road of Imperial Rome and there are some interesting remains.

Between Steinach and Gries there is a minor road giving direct access, via the hamlet of Vinaders, to the Obernbergtal with the hamlet of **Obernberg** strung out along the upper reaches. Beyond the guest house Waldesruh, where there is a large car park, the road is private and closed to traffic but it continues up to the

Obernberger See at 1,590m (5,215ft). It is a 45 minute walk up the road to the lake where there are good views. Nearby, but slightly higher, is the Seekappelle, lake chapel, which was built on its little hill in 1935. The path goes right round the lake and also continues south to the Portjoch, a pass on the Italian border. From here are extensive views of the peaks of the Dolomites and, just below, the Pflerschtal. The walk to the pass, which goes up to 1,836m (6,022ft) takes about $4^1/_2$ hours. On the lower parts there is a mixture of larchwoods and alpine meadows, while the paths are moderate and well marked.

From just below Gries there is yet another valley, this time going east, which divides at the hamlet of **St Jodok**. The southern spur goes to Valls, the northern to Schmirn and Kasern, while from Matrei there is a valley east to the village of Navis. All these side valleys are well off the tourist track though they do cater for visitors and nearly all have information offices so that one can find those delightful evening events which are so much a part of the Tyrolean scene. There are picturesque hamlets and pretty little churches and chapels all set against a backdrop of pinewoods and snowcapped mountains.

Not to be missed, even if the climb up the Brenner Pass is not attempted, is the **Ellbögen** road. Once this was a road used for the transporting of salt between Matrei and the main Inn valley. It is east, and on the other side of the River Sill, from the high road and the motorway. Passing the villages of Gedeier, where there is a campsite, and Mühlthal, the village of **Patsch** is soon reached where, on its southern outskirts, is a splendid view along the length of the Stubaital.

From here there is a road to **Igls**, a resort made popular since the 1976 Winter Olympic Games. It has a nine-hole golf course and sports facilities which reflect the closeness of Innsbruck which can be reached easily and quickly by frequent buses and trams. There is an indoor swimming pool but, in summer months, the favourite spot for swimming is at the small bathing lake, the Lanser See. It lies 1km ($^1/_2$ mile) from Igls on the edge of the plateau, while Igls itself lies back at the foot of the mountain.

However, the real lure is the cable car to the Patscherkofel. The valley station is at 903m (2,962ft) and there is an intermediate station, Heiligwasser (Holy Water) where the spring water is said to be a panacea for all ills, and which used to be very popular as

*Near the Mutterberg Alm in the Stubaital*

a place of pilgrimage. The highest station lies at 1,952m (6,402ft) where there is a hotel and restaurant. A chair lift continues on to the very summit at 2,246m (7,367ft) which is above the treeline and has spectacular views. North is Innsbruck and beyond the  Karwendel Mountains; north-west are the Meiminger Mountains and north of them the Zugspitze in the Wetterstein range marking the border with Germany. To the north-east, beyond the Karwendel group, the valley up to Achensee can be seen and beyond is the Rofan group. Countless glaciers can be seen to the south-west in the Stubaier Alps while south-east are the Tuxer Alps and, beyond, the peaks of the Zillertal Alps.

On the top there are many safe paths for an afternoon stroll taking in the views. A good walk may be made by first taking the cable car to the summit station where path 32 leads to the Bascheben Jausen-station (with a snack bar) on the Zirbenweg. There is a ridge path east then north, still on the Zirbenweg, and in the direction of the Viggarspitze. Path 48 forks left, north-east, off the Zirbenwag, then goes down via Isshutte to the Sistranser Alm, where refreshments are available. Path 49 leads to the Lanser Alm and path 4 to the Igler Alm and on to Heiligwasser where the cable car can be taken down again. The time for the walk is about 3 hours, easy going. The Igler Alm is a guest house and there is also a guest house at Heiligwasser.

The use of the word *Alm* is often misleading. It means 'Alp' or 'alpine pasture' and is dotted about quite frequently on detailed maps. Often there is a farmhouse and modern practice has turned this into a guest house. At a simpler, more remote, *Alm* the fare is simple — bread, cheese and beer, for example — but often an *Alm* will be a much grander affair more like a restaurant, especially where the tourist demand is being catered for.

## Additional Information

### Places of Interest

**Fulpmes**
*Forge Museum*
Exhibitions of tools
Open: Tuesday and Friday 4-6pm,
Sunday 10am-12noon.

### Tourist Information Centres

**Axams**
A-6094
☎ (5234) 8178, 7158

**Ellbögen**
A-6082
☎ (5222) 770 793

**Fulpmes**
A-6166
☎ (5225) 2235, 2892

**Gries**
A-6156
☎ (5274) 254

**Gries im Sellrain/Praxmar**
A-6182
☎ (5236) 224

**Igls**
A-6080
☎ (5222) 77101

**Kühtai**
A-6183
☎ (5239) 222

**Leutasch**
A-6105
☎ (5214) 6207, 6303

**Matrei**
A-9971
☎ (4875) 6527, 6709

**Mösern**
A-6100
☎ (5212) 8125

**Mutters**
A-6162
☎ (5222) 573744

**Neustift**
A-6167
☎ (5226) 2228

**Obernberg**
A-6156
☎ (5274) 532

**Patsch**
A-6082
☎ (5222) 77332

**Reith bei Seefeld**
A-6103
☎ (5212) 3114

**St Jodok**
A-6154
☎ (5279) 5204

**Scharnitz**
A-6108
☎ (5213) 5270

**Schönberg**
A-6141
☎ (5225) 2567

**Seefeld im Tyrol**
A-6100
☎ (5212) 2313, 2316

**Sellrain**
A-6181
☎ (5230) 244

**Stams**
A-6422
☎ (5263) 6511

**Steinach**
A-6150
☎ (5272) 6270

**Telfes**
A-6165
☎ (5225) 2750

**Telfs**
A-6410
☎ (5262) 2245

# 5
# *INNSBRUCK*

The city of **Innsbruck** ('bridge over the Inn') received its charter in 1239. It is the capital and cultural centre of the Tyrol and is reputed to be one of the most beautiful towns of its size in the world. The old part of the city is closed to traffic from 10.30am, allowing the visitor to appreciate the beauties without the attendant risk and annoyance from cars.

Innsbruck is young compared with Wilten, which is now a suburb of the town. According to legend in the sixth century the giant Raymon killed his rival Thyrsus near Seefeld. He was overcome by remorse and, having long admired the Benedictines of Tegernsee, he decided to build a monastery. Using blocks of limestone left by the Romans at their old town of *Veldidena* (Wilten), he proceeded to build. But work was sorely hampered by a dragon which playfully pulled down the stones by wrapping its tail around them and the workmen begged Raymon to deal with the fearsome monster. Raymon chased the dragon into a cave and killed it in masterly fashion.

Innsbruck itself began in 1180 when Count Berthold of Andechs bartered with Wilten Abbey for the land on which now stands the old centre of Innsbruck. The existing village was developed into a market town. A possible part of the price was a chalice and paten which became two of Wilten's greatest treasures and are now housed in a museum in Vienna.

In the twelfth century Innsbruck was an important trading post, no doubt partly because it commanded one of the most important trade routes across the Alps. Boats travelled up the Inn to Hall in Tyrol before unloading. This is only a few kilometres

downstream from Innsbruck and many of the goods travelled up to the Arlberg or up to the Oberinntal and into the Swiss Engadine. Traffic from Germany came this way over the Scharnitz and Brenner passes.

Prosperity increased when, in the early fifteenth century, Duke Friedrich transferred his official residence from Meran thus making Innsbruck the official capital of the Tyrol.

At the southern end of Maria Theresa Strasse stands the **Triumphal Arch**. In 1767 the imperial family were celebrating the marriage of Leopold, Grand Duke of Tuscany, to Maria Ludovica, the Infanta of Spain. Unfortunately, the Emperor Franz, husband of Maria Theresa, died suddenly during the celebrations. This is why, on the southern face of the arch the sculptured reliefs commemorate the marriage, while those on the northern face commemorate the funeral.

North from the Triumphal Arch, one of the most famous views

*The Goldenes Dachl with its golden tiles*

*The Hofburg, Innsbruck*

in Europe may be seen from half way up the street: it is best seen from the left-hand side. This view is of the Nordkette, the chain of peaks of the Karwendel mountains, and is a most impressive sight to suddenly behold in the centre of a city.

The column in the centre of the street is Annasäule or **St Anne's Column**, commemorating 26 July 1703 when an invading force of Bavarians retreated during the War of the Spanish Succession. Place of honour on top of the column is given to The Virgin while round the base are the figures of Saints Anne (on whose birthday the retreat occurred), George, Vigilus and Cassianus.

Straight ahead is Herzog Friedrich Strasse, a busy street with arcades of shops, at the end of which is the **Goldenes Dachl** or Golden Roof. This charming and unique balcony, with its golden roof, was built in 1500 on the instructions of Maximilian I as a place of comfort and as a vantage point from which to view the dancing in the square below. For centuries a tradition existed that the structure was built by Archduke Friedrich, nicknamed Friedrich the Penniless, to put an end to the jokes about his poverty. It is quite a sight to see the roof reflecting the sunlight. The Olympiamuseum (Olympic Museum) is housed here with exhibits of the Olympic Winter Games between 1964 and 1976.

Almost opposite is the **Stadtturm** (City Tower), a belfry standing alongside the old town hall. An octagonal Renaissance structure, rising from a square base, it bristles with turrets and is surmounted by a dome and lantern. The tower is open to the public and an English language brochure is available.

Look towards the Golden Roof and, on the left corner, is the **Helblinghaus** (number 10 Herzog-Friedrich Street). The house was originally late Gothic, about 1730. All the façades were covered with lavish late Baroque stucco work by Gigl Wessobrunner. The oriel shows late Gothic coats of arms reliefs by Gregor Türing. The Rococo facing with its lavishly decorated window frames, was added in the eighteenth century. The bow windows are in a style often seen in Southern Germany as a remedy for the darkness of narrow city streets.

A little further on, on the left, is the Goldener Adler (Golden Eagle), a well known old inn, with its marble plaque listing the famous guests it has received since the sixteenth century.

At the other end of the street is the **Hofburg**, a building erected piecemeal by the Habsburgs from the fifteenth century. It was almost completely restyled by the Empress Maria Theresa in the latter part of the eighteenth century. It was here that her husband died during the marriage festivities of their daughter in 1765. The two towers flanking the palace were finished in 1770. The state rooms are open to the public, with guided tours in English. Of particular interest is the Riesensaal (Giants' Hall) 31m (102ft) long, lined with stucco panels, and with its ceiling painted in 1776 by Franz Anton Maulpertsch. Its theme is the triumph of the House of Habsburg and is typified by two women holding out their hands to each other. Paintings on the wall are of Maria Theresa's children, other relatives and descendants, including Louis XVI and Marie Antoinette.

To the rear of the Hofburg is the **Dom zu St Jakob** (Cathedral of St James), which was rebuilt in the early eighteenth century. The old town surrounds the cathedral, making a most colourful picture with its ancient balconied houses.

Across the road from the Hofburg is the **Hofkirche** or Court Church, which was built in 1553-63 solely as a great mausoleum for the Habsburg Emperor Maximilian I. The building is in Gothic style, though the tower and entrance porch are Renaissance and there are Baroque additions dating from the early eighteenth century. The church is dominated by twenty-eight larger-than-life bronze statues of the emperor's ancestors plus notable kings, queens and emperors of history who stand guard around the tomb. Many are in elaborate suits of armour, as Innsbruck was a great centre of armour makers. Two of the statues — the legendary King Arthur of England and Theoderick, King of the Goths — were both sculpted by Albrecht Dürer. Ironically the remains of the emperor do not lie in his fabulous tomb — he is actually buried near Vienna, although the church does house the body of Andreas Hofer, the Tyrolean hero. The adjoining Silver Chapel with its silver Madonna was built in 1587 as a mausoleum by Archduke Ferdinand, the Regent of Tyrol. On the gallery there are twenty-three statues of the protecting saints of the Habsburg family.

The **Hofgarten** (Imperial Garden), near the Hofburg, offers the chance to relax with its shady walks, lakes and weeping willow trees. In summer months there are evening concerts.

Innsbruck has four main museums. The **Tiroler Volkskunst-museum** (Museum of Tyrolean Folk Art) displays an insight into

*A quiet drink at the Goldener Adler, Herzog-Friedrich Strasse in the old part of Innsbruck. In the distance is the Golden Roof*

*A golden eagle at the Alpine Zoo, Innsbruck*

the life of the region in bygone times, with examples of rooms both richly panelled from the homes of the wealthy and from those of the peasant. Also on display are examples of animal stalls, domestic utensils, games, tools, musical instruments, furniture, textiles and looms, glass and pottery. On the first floor is a collection of model houses, with the stone buildings of the Upper Inn valley and the wooden ones of the Zillertal. Not least is an extensive collection of peasant costumes, including those used at the Imst, Telfs and Nassereith carnivals (see Chapter 3). An English language brochure is available.

The **Tiroler Landesmuseum** (Museum of Fine Art) is concerned with the development of the fine arts in the Tyrol and has many paintings, woodwork and minerals, and sections devoted to the history of the Tyrol and of mountain buildings.

The **Kaiserjäger Museum** (Imperial Light Infantry Museum) on the Bergisel is the memorial to the Imperial Light Infantry, traces the history of the corps with uniforms, arms and paintings and also contains mementoes of the 1809 uprising. On the ground floor is a memorial to World War I. The corps was disbanded in 1919. From many of the windows there are good views of the town and of the mountains of the Nordkette.

An interesting hour can be spent in the **Alpenvereins Museum** (Alpine Club Museum) at Wilhelm-Greil-Strasse 15 is where there are relief maps of the famous mountain regions, old mountaineering equipment and clothing. There are also paintings, many by an Englishman, Edward Theodore Compton who was born in Stoke Newington in 1849. He moved to Germany with his parents in 1866 and a mountain holiday the following year inspired him to take up mountaineering and to indulge his passion for painting. He is credited with many climbs and some first ascents and it is estimated that he completed between 1,500 and 1,700 paintings, some of which were exhibited at the Royal Academy. He has been awarded the ultimate accolade for a mountaineer — a hut near Lienz named the E.T. Compton Hut.

In the suburb of **Wilten** the *Stiftkirche*, or abbey church, is well worth visiting. It dates from the seventeenth century but was restored in 1944 after it had been damaged. Two stone giants guard the doorway. The narthex or vestibule is enclosed by a magnificent grille dating from 1707 and contains another statue representing a giant, this time in wood and reputed to be

Raymon, founder of the abbey. The series of altar pieces, the paintings and the work above the high altar are all worthy of closer inspection.

Almost across the road is **Wilten Basilica**. The monastery had the parish church of Wilten completely restored between 1751 and 1756 in order to perpetuate the devotions to Our Lady of the Four Columns, who had been the object of pilgrimage to the area since the Middle Ages. In 1957 the church was raised to the status of basilica. Inside are a great many works by the artists of the Rococo period and, at the high altar, the statue of the Virgin, object of the pilgrimages.

South of the motorway, which is close by, is **Bergisel**. On the wooded hill are several monuments beside pleasantly laid-out walks. This was the scene of a battle in 1809 in which the hero of the Tyrol, Andreas Hofer, defeated the French invaders. Hofer became a larger-than-life folk hero and tributes to him may be seen throughout the Tyrol. After the War of Liberation the hill became a rifle range used by the Kaiserjäger but at the end of the century it became a Field of Remembrance. The monuments not to be missed include the Provincal Cenotaph and the Tomb of the Unknown Soldier. There is also a small lookout tower. With its beautiful woods and lawns, Bergisel is a favourite among the locals who come in search of peace and relaxation. In the background is the ski jump built for the 1964 Olympic Games.

On the opposite side of the city is the **Bergisel Riesenrundgemälde**. This huge circular fresco was painted in honour of Andreas Hofer and depicts the Battle of Bergisel in 1809.

Near the memorial is the **Hungerberg**. One of Innsbruck's favourite outings is to this area which may be reached by rack and pinion railway. From here a cable car ascends to the Hafelekar, (2,334m, 7,656ft) in two stages. The city lies at the foot of the mountain directly below while to the south are the southern ranges with glaciers as far as the eye can see. To the north are the Karwendel Mountains with the highest point, the Birkkarspitz, at 2,756m (9,040ft). There are safe well-defined footpaths to stroll along and mountain hotels for refreshment. Cable cars leave almost hourly from 8.15am in the summer season.

Another outing from Innsbruck is **Schloss Ambras**. Buses run from Innsbruck to the village of Ambras half-hourly for the half-hour trip. This magnificent castle is one of the best-preserved in

Austria. There has been a castle on this site since the eleventh century, but was completely rebuilt by Archduke Ferdinand. The family moved in in 1576 but building went on for about 20 years. The Spanish Hall, built in 1570, is the earliest known large Renaissance hall in the German speaking countries.

One thing which invariably remains in the memory of visitors to the castle is of Phillippine Wetser's bath. It was copper lined, measuring 2m (7ft) by 3m (10ft), and took about 900 litres (200 gallons) of water. Phillipine and Archduke Ferdinand II were married in secret in 1557 and the unfortunate lady lived under a cloud, though she was said to be happy. A marriage without parental consent was invalid under imperial law and, although Ferdinand's father forgave the couple, he insisted that the marriage should remain secret in view of the fact that Phillipine was a commoner. This meant that, although she was the Archduke's legal wife, the world thought of her as his mistress. Even after her death there was mystery. Rumour spread, as late as 1705, that she had been murdered in the giant bath: in truth she had died in bed, with her husband beside her. In 1889 an eminent historian complained to the Austrian Historical Society that visitors to the castle were still being told of the murder. Her memory is still revered by the people of Innsbruck.

The castle is almost two groups of buildings: the lower castle including the entrance lodge, and the upper castle, site of the former medieval fortress. A great part of the Archduke's personal collection was transferred, long ago, to Vienna but there is still an impressive display of weapons and armour along with equipment for jousting. There is also a collection of rare objects ranging from animal to mineral. Other exhibits include household gadgets and curios dating from medieval times.

The grounds of the castle are extensive and well laid out. They contain the original jousting area and, deep in the woods, a small cemetery in which lie heroes of the War of Liberation. Five guided tours, the first at 10am, take about $1^1/_4$ hours. This is a day's outing and well worth the time spent.

A pleasant short outing from Innsbruck is the **Ehnbach-Klamm** which is near Zirl. Here, through a wild gorge, a pathway has been carved through the rocks making a fine attraction.

The **Alpenzoo** (Alpine Zoo) is of interest to children and adults  alike. It is open all year, daily from 9am, and can be reached by bus from Maria Theresa Strasse, or by a comfortable half-hour walk. The zoo houses a wide variety of alpine animals and birds: marmot, beaver, vulture, eagle, eagle-owl, lizard, snake, and many more. In the mountains of Austria the fortunate walker, if out early enough and walking quietly, may see a chamois nearby or even watch an eagle soaring; after rain lizards bask on quiet high paths. But here at the zoo all may be seen at close quarters.

Innsbruck also has facilities for riding, an eighteen-hole golf course and an indoor swimming pool.

The road east from Innsbruck leads to **Hall in Tyrol**, 7km (4 miles) away. An observant citizen in 1280 observed a deer licking a rock near Hall and from this the Hall salt industry was born. At one time its population was larger than that of Innsbruck, but the choice of the latter as a centre of government and imperial residence meant that Hall ceased to expand.

No-one quite knows why this medieval town grew up so close to Innsbruck. Was it because this was where the river became navigable? There is just as much water at Innsbruck, and Innsbruck was where the first bridge was built, but Hall became the place where the great river boats stopped to unload. Up to twenty horses drew these boats, which often had smaller craft in tow. The journey upstream from Kufstein took 5 days but the return journey only 6 hours. Only small craft went up, past Innsbruck, to Telfs. Goods also came upstream on log rafts; after the goods were unloaded, the rafts were dismantled and used for firewood to stoke the boilers of the salt industry.

The old mint in Hall was founded in 1477. Rich finds of silver had been made in the mines at Schwaz, 30km (19 miles) east along the valley, and this made the journey to the old mint at Meran inconvenient. Added reasons were the distrust of the Swiss, and the Turkish incursions to the south, both nations possibly having designs on the old mint. Austrian patriots like to point out that the word 'dollar' originated from the Taler which took its name from the Inntal.

Hall in Tyrol has a splendid medieval 'old town'. The Unterer Stadtplatz is an open space formed by the main road but the main place of interest is the beautiful Oberer Stadtplatz (upper town square). This is not a square but an irregular space bounded by several picturesque and interesting buildings. Radiating from it are several beautiful streets.

The *Rathaus*, or town hall, is a building with a high roof. The main part of the building is sixteenth-century and carries some delicately carved designs and the statue of a knight with the coat of arms of Austria and the Tyrol.

The *Statdpfarrkirche*, or parish church, dates from the fifteenth-century and is surrounded by additions and annexes, including the chapel of St Joseph, and another dedicated to the Knight Florian Waldauf. Along with the Herz Jesus Basilica this is well worth visiting.

The best time to visit the Oberer Stadtplatz is on a Saturday when it is closed to traffic. Leave by way of the Rosengasse which leads towards the Stiftsplatz, where buildings are in a classical arrangement in contrast to the old town. They form a square and were formerly a convent, a church, and a college for Jesuits. Nearby is the Damestift (Ladies' Abbey) which was founded in 1567 by Archduchess Magdalene who is remembered by the statue in the square.

Forming a half circle to the north and west are magnificent boulevards known as the Staftgraben, which helps make this small town attractive. Hasegg Castle is home to a museum which houses exhibits of old life styles and houses and also of the salt workings. Between the river and the Unterer Stadtplatz is Münzergasse with the lovely old tower, the Münzerturm. There is an open air swimming pool and a campsite nearby.

This jewel of a town, set between the river and the mountains, is surrounded by meadows and there are some small villages nearby to explore. From Tulfes, to the south, a cable car ascends offering splendid views of this wider part of the valley.

An interesting walk from Hall in Tyrol is to take any of the side roads north to Absam, then to go by way of the guest house 'Walder Brucke' and on to the Walder Kapelle. From here the Egholungsweg goes through the woods to St Martin where there is an interesting church. The Waldlepfad leads on in the same direction to the next hamlet, St Michael. There is a south turn to Fritzens which soon joins a road but there is a right turn, westerly, to follow a track just south of the woods to Baumkirchen. Here another track just south of the woods leads to Grüneck and back to Hall. The route is just over 16km (10 miles) and there is an ascent of about 300m (984ft); the route is well served with places for refreshment.

Another interesting walk from Hall is to follow Lendgasse from the Unterer Standtplatz, cross the railway and follow the road to where it recrosses. Do not cross the railway again but take the path near the river, downstream. Cross the river by the road bridge, returning the same way. The round trip is 6km (4 miles), mostly on flat ground.

The Servitenkirche, or Servites Church, which is on this route, is a fine example of Baroque art. The church was completed in 1654 and is built round a central clover-leaf rotunda. The clock tower was added in 1740. From the bridge there is a good view of the whole church. A passageway links the church to the monastery, which is now a seminary for the Servites, a religious order who consecrate themselves to the upkeep of the pilgrimage sanctuaries in Austria. Dividing grilles bar much of the church but glimpses of fine paintings may be seen. The painting over the altar is of St Charles Borromeo who was the patron of the church.

The old road rather than the motorway is a more attractive route to the east. Volders, Wattens and Weer, where there is a camp site, all lie along this road. At the hamlet of Pill 3km (2 miles) further along, there is another camp site which is only 3km (2 miles) from Schwaz. All lie on the bus route along the main road and on the railway line.

**Schwaz** is interesting as it was hereabouts that rich finds of silver were made in the fifteenth-century. For a hundred years the mines were in full production and the town was very prosperous indeed. At the time it had the highest population of any town in the Tyrol apart from Innsbruck.

There are several interesting buildings in and around the town. In the summer there are weekly concerts in the hall of the cloisters of the Franciscan Monastery. The cloisters, open to view from the south side of the church, are pure Gothic in style with the remains of wall paintings dating from the sixteenth-century. Various shields of craft guilds and miners' guilds are shown as well as paintings on the vaulting dating from the seventeenth-century.

The Franziskanerkirche (Franciscan Church) was finished in 1515 and is laid out with three naves in accordance with the Order's own building rules. A notable feature is the Renaissance stall dating from 1618, which is the work of a local craftsman.

As befits a once prosperous town, the parish church reflects that prosperity. Dating from the fifteenth-century it was restored early in the twentieth century to its original Gothic style with network vaulting. There are four aisles and two chancels. Of particular interest is the elaborate Gothic decoration of the vaulting supporting the organ loft. The Baroque organ case is beautiful and the font dates from 1470. In the south aisle there is a very fine piece of religious sculpture, the altar of St Anne, dating from 1733, with St George and St Florian, the patron saints of Austria, framing a sixteenth-century group of the Holy Family with St Elizabeth and St Ursula. The church has two west doors, one of which was for the exclusive use of the miners.

On the outskirts of the town, to the south-east, is Schloss Freundsberg. This attractive castle, sitting boldly on the castle mound, is now the town museum with exhibits tracing the history of Schwaz and of the mining industry.

Open-air and covered tennis courts are available and there is a heated open air swimming pool. Riding facilities may be found in the nearby hamlet of **Pill**. A chair lift in three stages goes up to the nearby summit of Kellerjoch (2,344m, 7,688ft). The local council maintain 50km (30 miles) of footpaths for visitors.

## *Additional Information*

### *Places of Interest in Innsbruck*

**Alpenzoo** (Alpine Zoo)
In the Hungerberg area. Easily reached on foot in 30 minutes. Bus service from town centre.
Open: daily 9am-6pm.

**Dom zu St Jakob**
(Cathedral of St James)
Open: 6am-12noon, 2-5pm. Closed Friday and Sunday, also holiday mornings.

**Hofburg** (Imperial Palace)
Open: May to September 9am-5pm; October to April 9am-12noon and 2-5pm. Guided tours in English last 35 minutes.

**Hofkirche** (Court Church)
Open: May to September 9am-5pm; October to April 9am-12noon and 2-5pm.

**Schloss Ambras**
Open: mid-June to September, daily 2-6pm.

**Stadtturm** (City Tower)
Open: 1 March to 31 October 9am-5pm.

**Tiroler Landesmuseum**
(Museum of Fine Art)
Open: May to September, Monday to Saturday 10am-5pm, Thursday evening 7-9pm; Sunday and holidays 9am-12noon; October to April Tuesday to Saturday 10am-12noon, 2-5pm. Sunday and

holidays 9am-12noon. Closed on Monday.

**Tiroler Volkskunstmuseum**
(Museum of Tyrolean Folk Art)
Next to the Hofkirche
Open: weekdays 9am-12noon and 2-5pm. Sundays and holidays 9am-12noon.
English brochure available.

## Other Places of Interest

**Hall in Tyrol**
*Hasegg Castle*
Houses town and mining museum
Open: mid-June to September
Guided tours at 9.45am, 10.45am, 2.30pm, 3.30pm, 4.30pm. Mining museum, 10am, 11am and hourly 2-5pm.

**Schwaz**
*Schloss Freundsberg*
South-east of the town near church
Open: April to October, 10am-5pm.

## Innsbruck: Useful Information

**ACCOMMODATION**
*Youth Hostels*
**Youth Hostel Reichenau**
Reichenauer Strasse 147
☎ 46 179
Open: all year except 24 to 26 December.

**Youth Hostel Torsten-Arneus-Schwedenhaus**
Rennweg 17b
☎ 25 814
Open: July and August.

**Youth Hostel St Paulus**
Reichenauer Strasse 72
☎ 44 291
Open: mid-June to mid-August.

*Camping*
**Camping site Reichenauer Strasse**
☎ 46 252

**Camping site Innsbruck-West**
Kranebitter Allee 214
☎ 84 180

**Camping site 'Seewirt'**
Geyrstrasse 25
☎ 46 153
The tourist information centres publish a brochure *Innsbruck Hotel Price List* and *Igls Price List*.

**BANKS / EXCHANGING MONEY**
There are 10 banks with about 25 branch offices in all parts of the town.
Open: Monday to Friday, 7.45am-12.30pm and 2.30-4pm.

*Money Exchange*
Städisches Verkehrsbüro (tourist office)
Burggraben 3
Open: Monday to Friday 8am-12noon and 2-5.30pm, Saturday 9am-12noon.

*Money Exchange Central Station*
Open: daily 7.30am-8.30pm.
A money exchange service is also offered in most hotels and all travel agencies.

**CAR BREAKDOWN SERVICE**
ÖAMTC
Andechsstrasse 81
☎ 44 521
For breakdowns ☎ 44 154, emergency number 120

ARBÖ
Stadlweg 7
☎ 45 123

## CAR RENTAL

*Ajax Unfallhilfe*
Amraser Strasse 6
☎ 31 491

*Avis*
Salurner Strasse 15
Tourist Centre Holiday Inn
☎ 31 754

*Denzel*
Gumppstrasse 82
☎ 45 441

*Europcar (Ruefa Reisen)*
Salurner Strasse 16
☎ 32 151

*Hertz*
Stüdtiroler Platz 1
☎ 20 901

*Inter Rent*
Amraser Strasse 84
☎ 43 161

## EMERGENCY NUMBERS
Ambulance: 144 (in emergencies
only), otherwise 24 444
Fire brigade: 122
Police: 133
Mountain Rescue Service: 194

## HOSPITAL
*Allgemeines Öffentliches Landes-
krankenhaus (Universitätsklinik)*
Anichstrasse 35
☎ 26 711 or 28 711

*Hospital 'Sanatorium der
Barmherzigen Schwestern'*
Sennstrasse 1
☎ 37 511

## LEFT LUGGAGE OFFICE
Central Railway Station
Open: daily round the clock.

## LOST PROPERTY OFFICE
Bundespolizeidirektion (Police
Station) Innsbruck
Kaiserjägerstrasse 7
☎ 26 721

## PARKING
There is a parking fee in the town
centre's short term parking zones
(marked by special signs). Parking
vouchers can be bought in all post
offices, at most tobacconists,
automatic machines and at the
Städtisches Verkehrsbüro (tourist
office), Burggraben 3.

*Multi-storey and underground car
parks:*
Hotel Maria Theresia, Erlerstrasse
Sparkassen-Garage,
Sparkassenplatz 1

Garage Tourist Centre Holiday Inn,
Salurner Strasse 15

Markthallen Garage, Herzog-
Sigmund-Ufer

Garage Tiroler
Gebeitskrankenkasse, Klara-Pölt-
Weg 2.

## POLICE
Bundespolizeidirektion Innsbruck
Kaiserjägerstrasse 2
☎ 26 721

## POST OFFICES
*Hauptpostamt (Central Post Office)*
Maximilianstrasse 2
Open: Monday to Sunday round
the clock.

*Post Office Brunecker Strasse 1-3*
Open: Monday to Saturday
6.30am-9pm.

SIGHTSEEING TOURS

Short sightseeing tour of Innsbruck (duration about 1 hour) — bus leaves from Hofburg (Court Castle) at 10.15am, 12noon, 2pm and 3.15pm.
Special sightseeing tour (duration about 2 hours) — bus leaves from Bozner Platz at 10am and 2pm.

SHOPPING

In general, the hours of business are: Monday to Friday 8.30am-12noon and 2-6pm (groceries from 8am-12noon and 3-6.30pm), Saturday 8am-12noon. Closed on Sundays and bank holidays. Some shops and cafés, however, do not close for lunch.

TAXI

Taxi stands in all parts of the town, radio taxi ☎ 27711 or 45500.

TELEPHONE

The telephone code for Innsbruck from Austria is 052 22.

TOURIST INFORMATION CENTRES

*Städtisches Verkehrsbüro*
Burggraben 3
6020 Innsbruck
☎ 052 22/25 715

*Verkehrsamt Igls*
☎ 052 22/77 101

*Hotel Information*
Central Railway Station
☎ 052 22/23 766 and travel agencies.

THEATRE, MUSIC AND THE ARTS

*Concerts and Music Shows*
In the Kongresshaus (Convention Centre), Stadtsäle, Olympia-Eisstadion, Konservatorium (music school) and Schloss Ambras. For detailed information see the brochure *Innsbrucker Veran-staltungskalender* (*What's on in Innsbruck*) and daily newspapers.

*Folklore*
Tyrolean evenings in front of the Goldenes Dachl and in the following hotels: Adambräu, Hotel Sailer, Hotel Holiday Inn, Stifts-keller. Concerts of folk music in the music pavilion of Hofgarten and in the Schulgarten in Igls.
Regular parades of brass bands in traditional national costumes in Innsbruck and Igls.

*Galleries*
For addresses and dates of exhibitions consult the brochure *Innsbrucker Veranstaltungskalender.*

*Theatre*
Tiroler Landestheater and Kammerspiele, Rennweg. Pro-gramme information ☎ 217 71/01. Advance booking office ☎ 217 71/30. Volksbühne Blaas (Folk Theatre) in Gasthof Breinössl, Maria-Theresien-Strasse 12, ☎ 24 165
Alt-Innsbrucker Bauerntheater (Folk Theatre) in Gasthof Bier-stindl, Klostergasse 6, ☎ 24 960
Innsbrucker Kellertheater (Avantgarde Theatre), Adolf-Pichler-Platz 8, ☎ 20 743
For the programmes consult the daily newspapers or the brochure *Veranstaltungskalender.*

## Other Tourist Information Centres

**Hall in Tyrol**
A-6060
☎ (5223) 6269, 6220

**Schwaz / Pill**
A-6130
☎ (5242) 3240

# 6

# JENBACH AND THE
# ZILLERTAL

By way of the main road 171, or the minor road through the hamlets of Buch and Schlierbach, by rail or bus, **Jenbach** is not far from Schwaz. It is an unremarkable town not even listed in many guides, possibly because of its proximity to other more famous places such as Innsbruck, Achensee and Mayrhofen. It lies just north of the motorway, has an open air swimming pool, main line trains and buses. The town is at an important crossroads. South is the Zillertal, well known to many British holiday makers, while north is the Achental, a beautiful valley going up to the German border at the Achen Pass.

The journey up to the valley, which levels off after the 400m (1,312ft) climb from Jenbach, can be made by bus, train or road. Jenback in the main Inn valley lies at 562m (1,843ft) and the surroundings of the lake, up to the hamlet of Achental, are at about 920m (3,018ft).

There is a delightful narrow gauge rack and pinion railway, steam hauled, which runs between its own station, alongside the main line railway station in Jenbach, and the lakeside station 2km (1 miles) short of Pertisau. Buses run from Jenbach to the German border.

This hanging valley is of interest to geographers, for the waters drain north into the Isar and not south into the Inn. A barrier of glacial moraine, created when the Inn valley was carved by its glacier, is the explanation.

There are at least four camp sites around the Achensee and five spots from which lake bathing is possible. Steamers ply the full length of the lake which is the largest, and some say the most

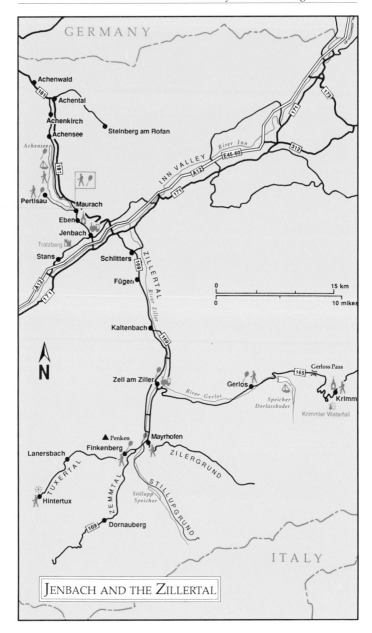

JENBACH AND THE ZILLERTAL

*Passenger ferry on the Achensee*

*The terminus of the Achensee narrow-gauge steam railway at Jenbach*

beautiful, in the Tyrol. It is almost 10km (6 miles) long and 1km ($^1/_2$ mile) wide at its widest point. In places it is nearly 150m (492ft) deep and the massive mountains of the Karwendel, to the west, and the Rofans, to the east, rise almost from the shores.

On the way up, splendid views down the Inn valley unfold while, higher up, mountain views are revealed. Lying off the main road, 181, is the tiny hamlet of **Eben**, with its church of St Norburga, Tyrolean patron saint of servants.

Only 1km ($^1/_2$ mile) north is **Maurach**, in the area of which there are two campsites, facilities for all water sports, and an indoor swimming pool. Tennis, bowling, cycle hire and minigolf are also available. A small local map of the footpaths may be obtained from the information office. A cable car goes up from near the centre of the village, at 958m (3,142ft) to a height of 1,834m (6,015ft). Here the Rofan Mountain Hotel can be found and, alongside it, the Erfurter Hut, an alpine club hut. Both have sun terraces overlooking the lake. Once this height is reached there are some good paths around the summits, the highest of which is the Hochiss at 2,299m (7,540ft).

The main road to Germany goes along the eastern bank of the lake. The road on the western bank ends at **Pertisau**. The village stands on a level section of land just before the ends of two valleys. All watersports are available, including fishing, and lake steamers call at the pier. There is both indoor and outdoor tennis, and in the evenings one may play by floodlight. There is a nine-hole golf course in delightful surroundings.

Behind the village the walk up to the Falzturnalm, a guest house, is delightful. It is open woodland but more like a park. Seats are provided for resting in the shade of mature trees of all kinds. The really hardy can go on to the Gramaialm, a large hotel with a farm nearby, and then on to the Lamsenjochhütte (1,953m, 6,406ft). However, this is a long walk and is tough over the last stretch. Cars can be driven up to the Gramaialm, but buses turn round at Pertisau.

At the foot of the lake (remember that the water runs north into the Isar and Germany) is the village of **Achensee** which spreads along the old road. The new high road takes all the faster through traffic and joins at **Achenkirch**. There is a lovely campsite on the lakeside with its own bathing place. The villages have a total of twenty-five pensions and seven hotels.

There are the usual facilities for water sports including rowing boats (motor boats are prohibited on the lake) and there is tennis, minigolf, bowling, riding and fishing, either on the lake or the river, and plenty of local footpaths for which the information office will supply a map. There is also a chairlift which will quickly take visitors to a height of 1,400m (4,592ft) on the slopes of the Hochunutz (2,075m, 6,806ft). The town band plays on some evenings and the village is not short of general evening entertainments.

**Achental** is the next hamlet and here there is a junction. A road leads off to the east, to the tree-covered hills and to a haven of peace and tranquillity. **Steinberg am Rofan** is a hamlet set deep in the hills to the north of the Rofan Mountains. As there is no through road (there is a track out to the east which is just drivable) the village enjoys complete quietness. Of course your morning sleep may be disturbed by cow bells or a tractor engine but there are few other noises.

The last village is **Achenwald** and it is at this point that the road and river part. The road soon climbs to the Achen Pass, taking the easiest route northward, while the river takes the easiest way down. It flows into the Sylvenstein reservoir in Germany, which is on the course of the Isar.

One of those anomalies found in mountain country lies a little way west. By following the road past the reservoir to Vorderris and turning south, the hamlets of Hinterris and Eng can be reached. Though they are both in Austria the only road access is north through Germany.

**Hinterriss**, the occasional holiday venue of the Belgian royal family, has a few houses grouped around a nineteenth-century hunting lodge. The area is a nature reserve in which chamois may easily be seen. There is a modern guest house/restaurant and even a fuel station. Plenty of gentle footpaths go round the area at a modest level though there are also high level paths.

Higher up the Engtal is the hamlet of **Eng** itself. Here a collection of holiday chalets line the end of the road and there is a large guest house. There are many German visitors at weekends, climbing the good paths south-west to the Binns Alm or to the higher Lamsenjoch hut which stands at the head of the Falzturn valley south-west of Pertisau. *Joch* means 'pass' and from Eng the hut is just the other side of the Lamsenjoch, at

1,938m (6,357ft). To the west, along a good path, is the Falkenhut, a climb of 590m (1,935ft). This is a fine walk giving splendid views of some of the peaks of the Karwendel mountains and a massive limestone wall ahead soon after the start. The paths are good and safe and at all the huts and *Alms* refreshments and accommodation are available.

Back down in the main valley south-west of Jenbach on the old road to Stams is **Schloss Tratzberg**. This gem among castles must be visited. The beginnings of Tratzberg are almost in the realms of legend, the records are so few. The first mention was in 1149 when the Rottenburg masters were squires to the Counts of Andechs. Two brothers of the Rottenburg line disputed over which ruling house to follow — Habsburg or Bavaria. One took over Rottenburg, which is across the valley and now a ruin, while the other brother built Tratzberg, out of spite it is said; the name is derived from *trotzen* meaning 'to defy'.

In 1500 the old castle was pulled down and rebuilt. A stone-carved coat of arms in the tower stairway reads in translation: '1500 Veit Jakob and Simon Tänzl, brothers did build this castle'. However, their fortunes changed and the Ilsungs became the new owners. This latter family continued the lavish decoration, but with a difference — the Tänzls built and decorated in Gothic style, the Ilsungs in Renaissance. During a period when the Fuggers owned the castle they had the courtyard decorated. All the decorated façades are signed 'PD 1600' and are attributed to Peter Donner. In 1847 the castle finally passed into the hands of the Counts of Enzenberg, who still own it. It is thanks to them that previous neglect and decay has been halted and restorative work undertaken.

To visit the castle take the minor road from Jenbach to Stams, for 2km (1 mile) to the guest house Schlosshof. From here the visitor must take a 20-minute walk up a neat path through the woods past the outer bastions and terraces.

Part of the large castle is open to view but, even so, it is not possible to describe all that may be seen. The first room on view is the hunting room containing lifelike groups of animals carved by a local man from Achental, Toni Steger. Many of the rooms are named after the Fugger family, for instance the richly panelled Fugger parlour and Fugger chamber have furniture of interest. In the Habsburg hall, 16m (52ft) by 10m (33ft) are paintings of the

Habsburg family, 148 portraits in all. They are of great interest for the information they provide concerning the clothes of the sixteenth century.

Among other rooms is the queen's bedchamber, a room which illustrates the culmination of Renaissance splendour during the Ilsung family ownership. On the north-east corner is the castle chapel dedicated to St Catherine, consecrated in 1508. The altar painting is early Baroque and shows the beheading of St Catherine.

Finally, the armoury is visited. Prolific records trace the development of armoury. This is one of the largest in Austria although over the years many items have been lost in battle. Notable items are the two long chamois spears used by Emperor Maximilian. Tratzberg has a widespread reputation for its historical culture and is an experience not to be missed.

South of Jenbach is the Zillertal, one of the most delightful valleys and centres one could wish to find. For many years it has been a favourite with visitors from Britain and it is claimed to be

*The Zillertal, a typical Tyrolean valley*

the most typical Tyrolean valley. Musicians from the Zillertal were known in all the courts of Europe and a group appeared in London in 1837 to perform during Queen Victoria's Coronation celebrations. So captivated was the queen that many an English soprano found it expedient to learn the 'wild songs'. Today, its musicians are still famous for singing and for harp and zither playing. On the first weekend in May there is a spectacular festival, the Gauder Festival, which dates back over 400 years and thousands flock to watch and to join in.

Before 1805 the Zillertal was not in the Tyrol but came under the jurisdiction of the Bishops of Salzburg. Note the difference in the 'onion domes' of the churches: there is a boundary between the red and the green tops.

Higher up, beyond the Gerlos Pass, was a place famous for crystal and many folk tales tell of mountain caves lined with crystal. Aquamarines used to be found in the area, but the Zillertal was most famous for garnets.

The lower reaches of the valley are broad and may disappoint those expecting alpine scenery. First of the villages is Strass near Jenbach, then Schlitters and Fügen, Kaltenbach, Aschau and then Zell am Ziller.

Here the valley divides, the main valley going on to Mayrhofen while the offshoot goes to Gerlos. At Mayrhofen the valley again divides, this time into four. Mayrhofen is the start of picture postcard land again. Each of the side valleys cut deep into the Zillertal Alps and a high alpine road has been built to take motorists up to points for viewing many peaks over 3,000m (9,840ft)

**Strass** has the first railway station on the way up the valley. **Schlitters** has an open air swimming pool near the campsite.

**Fügen** is a few kilometres further up the valley, which is still wide at this point. Here there are facilities for tennis, minigolf and table tennis, a swimming pool and large sunbathing lawn near the campsite. Over 90km (56 miles) of paths are cared for with three hundred benches for resting and taking in the views. A cable car goes up south-west of the town taking the more adventurous up for an attempt on the Kellerjoch (2,344m, 7,688ft) or the Rastkogel (2,745m, 9,004ft). A cycle path, the Radwanderweg, has also been laid out. There are many hotels and pensions and an active night life.

**Kaltenbach** is another pleasant little village catering for winter and summer tourists.

For many the Zillertal starts at **Zell am Ziller**, a lovely little village situated where the valley begins to narrow. The high spot for railway buffs will be the old steam train, which sometimes has scheduled runs to Mayrhofen; it is even possible to rent the whole train.

Set in a wide open area is the heated open-air swimming pool with its lawns and there are facilities for tennis, open-air chess, fishing and cycle hire. There is an active night life with Tyrolean evenings, cellar bars, discotheques and brass band concerts.

**Mayrhofen** appears to have everything from a conference centre to a baby-sitting service, a cinema to a forest feast. In between there is fishing, swimming, tennis, riding, cycle hire and bowling. There is a good selection of evening entertainments at many of the local hotels and six *Tanzlokale*, places for dancing. The village claims to have 200km (124 miles) of footpaths.

A pleasant, easy 9km (6 mile) walk goes along the forest edge down to Zell am Ziller and takes about 2$^1/_2$ hours. One could arrange this to coincide with a return trip by steam train. The walk starts behind the Europahaus, the conference centre, and goes left at the end of Dursten Strasse. Follow a field path to Eckartau, down through the village, to a signposted track to Ramsau. Turn down into Ramsau and right at the church, where a track leads to Zell am Ziller.

A high level walk can be taken by using the cable car, Penkenseilbahn, to Gschössberg (1,787m, 5,861ft). From there, an easy 3-hour walk, mostly terraced at the top, gives splendid views of the valleys round Mayrhofen and the glaciers of the Zillertal Alps. A chair lift may be taken higher, to 2,005m (6,576ft), or footpath 23 near the cable may be followed. A ridge path then goes south-westerly to a minor summit and on to Penken (2,095m, 6,871ft). Behind the nearby Penkenjoch Hut the path turns slightly right and goes downhill, then forks to the left. A further left turn takes a path down to the Mösingalm and the middle station on the Finkenberg chair lift. The lift may be taken down to Finkenberg or the walk can be continued in this direction to the Penkenhaus (1,810m, 5,937ft). A good footpath goes on to the Gschosswand for a return by cable car. The walk takes 3 hours on easy paths. However, one must allow time for taking in the

⇐ *A winter scene near Mayrhofen looking towards the Branderberger Kolm*

*A typical Tyrolean* Gasthof *in Mayrhofen*

*Grinberg from the Penken-Alpe, near Mayrhofen*

splendid views. From the ridge on the higher sections of the walk there is a general panorama view of the Zillertal Alps.

**Finkenberg** is an attractive place to stay. Quieter than Mayrhofen, this little village is the home of Leonhard Stock, the world famous Olympic ski champion. It lies just inside the Tuxertal, the most westerly of the four fingers of the valleys, or grounds (*Gründe*), fanning out from Mayrhofen. Finkenberg has a heated open air pool, facilities for tennis and bowling, and, of course, the chair lift to the Penken. A walking programme is available from the information office. There are concerts and slide shows in the evenings.

Higher up the valley the village of **Lanersbach** has a cable car — it actually starts from the nearby hamlet of Vorderlanersback — which goes up to the Schrofen Hut at 1,700m (5,576ft).

**Hintertux**, at the head of the valley, is almost against the valley head wall. It is from here that the cable car goes up to the permanent glaciers and snowfields which provide all-year skiing. At an altitude of 2,660m (8,725ft) the Tuxer-ferner Haus has a terrace facing south to the snowfields. The experience of sunbathing beside a snowfield is one not be be missed; but remember to be extremely cautious when exposing skin in the thin air at this altitude. It will feel cool but the intensity of ultra-violet rays is much greater than most lowlanders are accustomed to. The village is a centre for traditional woodcarving and is also popular as a health spa; the swimming pool is a thermal pool.

All of this valley is a winter and summer paradise. Many of the hotels in the hamlets have sports facilities: one in the hamlet of Madseit near Hintertux has a bowling alley. Frequent bus services from Mayrhofen make access easy and an abundance of footpaths provide both low level strolls and harder high level hikes. The tourist office will provide sketch maps of the paths.

An interesting walk can be taken from Hintertux. First take the cable car to the Sommerbergalm at 2,080m (6,822ft) which is the changeover point for the higher section to the Tuxer-Ferner Haus. Either take the path to the Tuxer-Joch Haus, or the chair lift to the Tuxer Joch (2,338m, 7,669ft). Down the other side of this pass is Schmirn, in one of the side valleys of the Brenner Pass.) From the Tuxer-Joch Haus take path 323 down the Weitental, an area frequented by chamois. Lower down the stream plunges into a wild gorge where often a haze is thrown out by the waterfalls, making it very attractive. It is an easy 3-hour walk. The more energetic can use path 324 to walk all the way up from Hintertux; the ascent will take about 2 hours.

Beyond the village of Dornauberg the road goes through a series of tunnels, the first 3km (2 miles) long, and has a number of hairpin bends on its climb up to the large lake, Speicher Schlegeis at 1,780m (5,838ft). The entire length of this drive gives magnificent views of the highest peaks of the Zillertal Alps.  There is a car park beside the Dominikshütle, near the lake, where short strolls can be made to take in the scenery. The road round the lake is private but walking is allowed. This is a magnificent high alpine spot surrounded by peaks over 3,000m (9,840ft) high, snow-capped all year round. The Hochfeiler, 3,510m (11,513ft), is south, in line with the lake, while to the east is the Grossem Möseler, 3,478m (11,408ft).

Considered the most picturesque of the four 'grounds' is the Stilluppgrund. Buses run from Mayrhofen to the Grune Wand Haus at 1,438m (4,717ft) at the head of this valley, but cars are not allowed quite so far. A fast glacier-fed stream tumbles over many waterfalls in a gorge before the valley widens and gives views of the surrounding peaks and glaciers.

The Ziller river, from which the Zillertal derives its name, flows down the last valley (or 'ground'), the Zillergrund. Due east from Mayrhofen is the hamlet of Häusling, a few guest houses, and, at the roadhead, the Bärenbad Alm. This climbs amid magnificent scenery almost to the border of the neighbouring province of Salzburg.

At Zell am Ziller road 165 goes east towards Gerlos and the Gerlos Pass at 1,507m (4,943ft). Buses run from Zell am Ziller and special outings can be made to visit the Krimml Waterfalls.

From Zell the road starts off through the hamlet of Hainzenberg, which is reached by a series of hairpin bends up a steep slope. The Gerlos valley is a hanging valley and the route over the pass is classed as a scenic route, as, indeed, is the whole Zillertal.

**Gerlos** lies in a secluded combe at 1,245m (4,084ft). This beautiful high valley is popular both in winter and summer. Many visitors travel along this road which winds through pine forests and pastures. Accommodation is plentiful and there are comfortable walks through meadows and woods to the welcoming *Alms*.

*Skiing in the Tuxertal*

*Taking a break high in the mountains of the Tuxertal*

A chair lift goes up to the Ebenfelder Aste (1,820m, 5,970ft) from where the highest peak in the Kitzbüheler Alps may be ascended. Path D2 goes first to the Isskogel (2,263m, 7,423ft) and continues, taking a left fork to the Kreuzjoch at 2,559m (8,394ft). The return may be made the same way. The path is not too difficult and the start is over wonderful alpine pastures which are full of flowers in their season. Allow 6 hours for the round trip. Views from the summits are breathtaking. To the south-east is the Hohe Tauern range with many peaks over 3,000m (9,840ft)

Gerlos has four swimming pools, including a heated outdoor pool, and a tennis court. There is fishing and sailing, with boats for hire on the nearby lake, and beautiful side valleys to explore.

A wide sweep round the Durlassboden Dam starts the climb to the Gerlos Pass, with a second sweep climbing higher with a view over the lake. The actual Gerlos Pass lies on the minor road at 1,507m (4,943ft) from where a nearby chairlift ascends to the Konigsleiten. This was the original road but the new main tourist road goes even higher to the Filzsteinalpe (1,628m, 5,340ft) where there is a car park.

The road downwards is fast and round a series of hairpin bends. The first view is of the upper Pinzgau valley and, in particular, the Krimmler Waterfall. Next is a view of a landlocked lake, the Burgwandkehre, and its remarkable hillock, the Trattenköpf. Just as the road sweeps round to enter a tunnel there is a car park and a closer view of the falls.

It is possible to walk to the falls. Leave the car in **Krimml** to avoid a toll road. A broad path leads to the lower falls. The path climbs with many hairpin bends and side paths to viewing points of the cascades until, after about an hour's walking, a level pasture is reached for a welcome pause at the guest house Schönangerl. Another guest house, the Tauern Haus, stands at the top of the falls. The falls higher up are bigger than those before the Schönangerl and it is worth the extra effort to see them. Altogether the Krimml Falls descend about 383m (1,256ft) and are the highest in Europe. A raincoat is advisable as the woods are misted with spray from the huge cascades. At least $3^1/_2$ hours should be allowed for a full tour of the falls and the best views are obtained at mid-day when the sun is behind them.

Before leaving Krimml, a visit to the parish church is worthwhile in order to see the Madonna.

# Additional Information

## Places of Interest

**Schloss Tratzberg**
Jenbach, A6130 Schwaz, off the
minor road between Jenbach and
Stans.
Open: enquire at Jenbach tourist
office.

## Tourist Information Centres

**Achenkirch**
A-6215
☎ (5246) 6270

**Eben**
A-5531
☎ (6464) 8194

**Finkenberg**
A-6292
☎ (5285) 2673

**Fügen**
A-6263
☎ (5288) 2262

**Gerlos**
A-6281
☎ (5284) 5244, 5416

**Jenbach**
A-6200
☎ (5244) 3901, 3470

**Kaltenbach**
A-6272
☎ (5283) 2218

**Krimml**
A-5743
☎ (6564) 239

**Maurach**
A-6212
☎ (5243) 5340, 5355

**Mayrhofen**
A-6290
☎ (5285) 2305

**Pertisau**
A-6213
☎ (5243) 5260

**Schlitters**
A-6262
☎ (5288) 2847

**Steinberg am Rofan**
A-6215
☎ (5248) 321

**Strass**
A-6261
☎ (5244) 2144

*For Lannersbach & Hintertux*
**Tuxertal**
A-6293
☎ (5287) 606

**Zell am Ziller**
A-6280
☎ (5282) 2281

# 7
# AROUND THE
# GROSSGLOCKNER

The descent from the Gerlos Pass takes the road into Salzburg Province. However, a short detour enables one to visit the Grossglockner High Alpine Road — one of the engineering masterpieces of Europe. The Felber Tauern Tunnel takes the road back south into the East Tyrol.

Having left the Zillertal Alps behind, road 165 leads down the Oberpinzgau valley between the Kitzbühler Alps to the north and the Hohe Tauern to the south. The Hohe Tauern contains the highest mountain in Austria — the Grossglockner, 3,797m (12,454ft). Tours are available from the nearby towns or you may wish to drive over the magnificent high alpine road culminating in the pass at Hochtor, 2,505m (8,216ft).

From Krimml the first village is **Wald-im-Pinzgau** where, in the late Gothic churchyard, are many headstones made of rare minerals. The Pinzgau valley, with the young Salzach river, runs down to Mittersill. Swiftly growing in size, the Salzach flows on to the east for some hundred miles or so before swinging north through Bischofshoven, then Salzburg; a few miles north it forms the border with Germany, then flows into the River Inn which, in turn, after some 80km (50 miles) joins the Danube.

The Upper Pinzgau valley is an ideal holiday centre for those who cannot make up their minds whether to take a winter, spring, or summer holiday. When the main valley, the Salzachtal, is experiencing full summer with meadows clothed in flowers, the side valleys are just in spring, and the higher reaches are in permanent winter with snowcapped peaks and all-year skiing. It is quite possible to ski in the morning then to play tennis or to sail

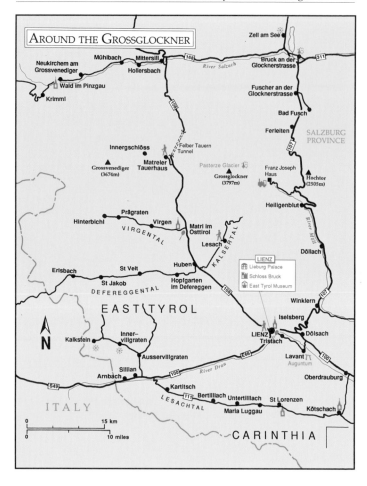

in the afternoon.

The road 165 goes through Vorder Krimml, Wald-im-Pinzgau, Rosenthal, Neukirchen-am-Grossvenediger, Habach, Bramberg-am-Wildkogel, Mühlbach, and Hollersbach before reaching Mittersill, which is just off a major crossroad.

**Hollersbach** and **Neukirchen am Grossvenediger** are main resorts for both winter and summer holidays with all the usual facilities. **Habach** is at the foot of one of the main side valleys

*A view down the Tauern Valley looking towards the Grossvenediger*

*Weissenstein Castle, Matrei in Osttirol*

which cut south, deep into the high mountains. The Habachtal is the valley where many emeralds were once found. Examples of these fine jewels can be seen in Salzburg Cathedral, in the Habsburg Crown Jewels in Salzburg Natural History Museum, and in the British Crown Jewels. Poor quality stones are still found although no fine emeralds have been discovered for many years and recent attempts to start new works have not met with success. The town is a winter and summer resort and has bus and rail links.

South of the town the main road 108 climbs up the Felber and Amer valleys. To the left is an are of wildlife park (*Naturschutz-park*). On both sides are breathtaking views of the Hohe Tauern range. Finally the road enters the Felber Tauern Tunnel.

In common with many tunnels and high alpine roads, a toll payment is required. The tunnels and high roads have, in many areas of Austria, been built mainly in response to the demand of tourism and trade. For example, much traffic flows through Austria en route from Northern Europe to the Middle East. Having been forced to build these roads and tunnels in order to stop traffic stifling the country, the authorities reason that the users should bear some of the cost. The tolls are quite heavy but, when compared with the cost of fuel for a diversion, not excessively so.

The Felber Tauern Tunnel is 5km (3 miles) long and is at an altitude of 1,600m (5,250ft). It makes the crossing from Salzburg Province into East Tyrol.

When the South Tyrol was given to Italy, the East Tyrol was cut off and isolated from the North Tyrol as the Grossglockner is closed in winter. For a long time the East Tyrol became a backwater and the scattered inhabitants had to deal with serious economic problems. However, the tunnel changed all that and visitors can now gain easy access all year round.

On emerging from the southern end of the tunnel there is a car park and, to the west up the valley, a magnificent view of the Grossvenediger (3,674m, 12,051ft). A little further down there is a right turn to the Matreir Tauern Haus, a mountain hotel, from where it is possible to take a stroll to visit the unusual chapel at Aussergschloss which is carved out of a large rock.

Continuing down the valley, which is the Tauerntal, beside the River Tauern, the next village is **Matrei in Osttirol**, a picturesque

town and a summer resort. The parish church is Baroque and
attributed to Haganauer. Nearby is Weissenstein Castle, formerly an outpost of the Bishops of Salzburg. In the thirteenth-
century church of St Nicholas (Nikolauskirche) are some of the
oldest preserved frescoes in Austria, also dating from the thirteenth-century.

Matrei is a centre for climbing; it has a campsite, swimming
pool and facilities for riding. It also lies at the junction of the
Tauern and Virgen valleys. Along this fine, unspoilt, and dramatic valley, which is only 17km (10 miles) long, lie the villages
of Virgen, Prägraten and Hinterbichl. At its highest reaches is the
birthplace of the River Isel and all around are peaks of over
3,000m (9,840ft). Post buses serve its villages, none of which
appear in tourist brochures and are visited only by the Austrians
and Germans for whom it is a few hours' drive away.

**Huben** stands guard at the next valley junction. Here are two
valleys, to the west the Defereggental, and to the east the
Kalsertal. **Kals** is the main village and is one of the leading centres
for climbing. At the very head of the valley is the Kalser Tauern
Haus, a mountain inn. From **Lesach**, the village below Kals, a
walk up the side valley to the Lesacher Alpe will reward the
energetic with beautiful unspoilt mountain scenery, but there are
no chair lifts or cable cars. From Kals to the Kalser Tauern Haus
the road climbs northward and the end of the road, at the inn, lies
beneath the western slopes of the Grossglockner.

Back towards the main valley through the village of Peischlach
and across the main road heading due west is the Defereggental,
cutting deep into the Defereggen Mountains. Soon after entering
the valley there is a chair lift going northward onto a ridge with
splendid views along the valleys and over the mountains.

**Hopfgarten in Defereggen** is the first village reached, followed by St Veit and St Jakob, a small winter and summer resort
and a marvellous example of a high mountain village.

**Erlsbach**, until recently, marked the end of the road: now,
however, it is possible to drive on, up to the Staller Sattel, where
there is a border crossing into Italy. The descent into Italy is very
steep and twisting. It is too narrow to allow two-way traffic but
a tidal flow system is in operation whereby, at alternate times,
one-way traffic is allowed to flow from either end.

It is possible to take a short cut back to Innsbruck. On joining the main road 49, turn right towards Bruneck, continue towards Brixen but turn onto road 12 at Schabs. This is the old road over the Brenner Pass and is much more interesting than the motorway, which is also a toll road.

Having turned left (east) back towards Austria and crossed the border, the villages of Arnback and Sillian greet the returning traveller into the Pustertal. The river in the valley is the Drau; it rises in Italy and, when it reaches Yugoslavia, becomes the Drava. The road is good and the valley broad. To the south are the Lienzer Dolomite Mountains while to the north are the Defereggen Mountains. On the south slope of the Defereggens a number of villages on a 'sun terrace' can be reached by a minor road. **Bannberg**, **Assling**, **Unterried** and **Anras** must be sought out on a good road map and the turning to them carefully looked out for, but it is worth the effort as they are typical unspoilt villages.

At the hamlet of **Panzendorf**, not far from the border, turn north for another of those romantic valleys. This one is the longest off the Pustertal, about 12km (7 miles) to the top. Pass through Ausservillgraten and take the right turn through Tilliach to the Sillianer Haus, a mountain inn at the head of this branch. The other branch of the valley is of roughly equal length and has the hamlets of **Innervillgraten** and **Kalkstein**, which is at the head of this branch and is in a loop of the Italian border. These picturesque villages, almost hidden from the rest of the world, are absolutely beautiful and almost entirely unspoilt.

Retracing ones steps towards the border, **Sillian** is the highest village and is almost at the frontier. Nearby is Heimfels Castle which is slowly decaying though a wander round the walls and courtyards is rewarding. It belonged to the counts of Görz and dates from the thirteenth-century.

Yet another dramatic valley lies within reach. Just beyond Pazendorf, on the way back down the valley towards Lienz, there is a turning to the right which leads up to **Kartitsch** and the remote valley of Lesach. To the north, though not in evidence, are the Lienzer Dolomites and to the south the Karnische Alps. The road is number 111 and leads eventually to Villach.

Beyond Kartitsch is the highest point of the valley and by the time Leiten is reached the River Gail is running in the same direction as the road, almost south-east. The river is well below the road, deep cut in the bottom of the valley, and there are reputed to be seventy-two ravines on its course. However, the road is high on the northern, or sunny, side and the ravines are far below. This means there are some very fine views of the valley from the road itself and these are best seen driving down the valley on the route described. There is a splendid double waterwheel near **Untertilliach**.

Altogether there are six villages in this beautiful valley which are certainly off the beaten track. Below Leiten, in order of appearance, are Obertilliach, Luggau, St Lorenzen, Kornet and St Jakob. From the pass summit it is 53km (33 miles) to Kötschach, in the course of which the route leaves the East Tyrol and enters Carinthia.

The border is hardly notable but the next village, **Luggau**, certainly is. At the pilgrimage church of St Maria Luggau testimonials from the many supplicants are on display, currently dated, and on either side of the village the stations of the cross line the road. The story, told in full in a series of picture boards in the cloisters, is that in 1513 a young woman had a dream which was followed by a number of miracles. The stations of the cross are repeated at St Jakob but this time leading up a grassy ridge to a chapel on a hill. There is a mill museum at Luggau.

Just outside the hamlet of **Birnbaum** is a small layby from where there is a good view south, across the river, to the hamlets of Woodmaier and Nostra. Even more remote is the hamlet of **Tuffbad** which can be reached by a very minor road turning left just as the outskirts of St Lorenzen are reached. It is claimed that in this remote corner of Carinthia more of the local colour and original costumes survive than anywhere else. The local summer festivals attract a wide local audience and Carinthian cooking specialities are renowned. It is also an area where the walking and climbing are superb. This valley has a happy and contented feel to it, giving a sense of wellbeing and calm.

At the twin resorts of Kötschach and Mauthen, once the last hairpin bends have been negotiated, there is a crossroads. East is the Gailtal and Villach: south is the Plocken Pass and Italy: north is the Gailbergsattel, leading back to the Drau valley and on towards Lienz. In **Kötschach** is a sixteenth-century church; its doorways and buttresses are made of the local red sandstone with intricate vaulting and groining typical of the late Gothic.

The main valley is reached once more at **Oberdrauburg**. Those with time to spare should not rush headlong back to Lienz but, soon after re-entering the East Tyrol, branch off to the right to Nikolsdorf and Lengberg to escape the traffic. Soon after being forced to rejoin the main road a left turn leads to Lavant and Tristach where the locals from Lienz spend summer weekends by the lakeside.

Near **Lavant**, archaeologists are excavating the Roman city of *Aguntum*. A splendid dig, it is the only one in the world being carried out with the aid of an original map. This map is on a sheet of lead, presumed to have been part of a roof. The layout of the streets and buildings can all be seen on this amazing relic of the past and enables the archaeologists to pinpoint the site over an extremely large area. At one time the city was larger and had many more inhabitants than present day Lienz but it was laid to waste, together with its nearby temple, in the fifth-century by the Avars and the Slavs. Details are still being discovered, but the ancient bishopric of *Aguntum* was last heard of in the year AD604.

**Lienz** is very old but has suffered six great fires in its history, the first in 1444 and the last in 1825. The town is delightful and is the shopping centre for the East Tyrol. The massive peaks to the north are dramatic yet Lienz gives the impression that southern Europe has been reached; visitors will be surprised to see palm trees growing in the street. It lies at an important junction, with the route north into the Isel valley and its side valley which is still today one of the few remaining really traditional and unspoilt valleys of the Austrian alpine area, and its other routes via the Hochpustertal into Italy, the high Grossglockner Pass, and the Drau valley.

Sights not to be missed in Lienz include the Lieburg Palace located in the main square. Dating from the sixteenth century it is now the seat of local administration.

Schloss Bruck, lies just outside the town and now houses the East Tyrol Museum (Osttiroler Heimatmuseum). It was probably built on the site of the Roman citadel which previously guarded the valleys. Dating from the thirteenth century, and partially restored in the sixteenth century, it is very well preserved. Exhibits include finds from the nearby Roman excavations, local antiquities, handiwork and folklore. Certainly not to be missed is the gallery in which are hung the paintings of Franz Defregger and Albin Eggar-Lienz. Inspired by the people and landscape of the Tyrol these brilliant painters have encapsulated a social history of the late nineteenth and early twentieth century. Other outstanding features are the tower, the Knights' Hall showing how the castle must have looked in medieval times, and the Romanesque Chapel. In the chapel are fifteenth-century frescoes by Simon von Taisten who worked on a number of churches in the Pustertal. The frescoes were commissioned by Count Leonhard and his wife Paula. Count Leonhard was the last of the line of the House of Görz and on his death the province passed to Emperor Maxmilian I, thus becoming part of the Tyrol.

In the parish church, which fortunately survived the disastrous fires, are the tombstones, in Salzburg marble, of the Count and his wife. Here, also are four late Gothic altars, and frescoes by Adam Molk.

Lienz has an information office and facilities for many sports. There is a cycle path, facilities for riding, bowling, tennis and minigolf. Walking is, of course, a great pastime and many paths extend from the outskirts of the town into the pleasant woods. It is a centre for climbing and is a winter sport centre.

Swimming is well catered for and Lienz claims to have the most modern facilities at the Dolmitenbad Lienz. Here there is a huge outdoor pool with large sunbathing lawns and a nearby indoor pool with a restaurant. Near the town is the small Tristach See, a lovely little lake with a lido providing facilities for bathing.

A cable car to the north-east ascends the slopes of the Zeltersfeld, 2,213m (7,258ft) and to the west a chair lift goes up the Hockstein. Good footpaths and mountain inns make walking in these mountains delightfully comfortable.

By taking road 107 out of Lienz the border with Corinthia is soon reached at the Iselsberg Pass (1,204m, 3,950ft), but first one finds the village of **Iselsberg** which is a winter and summer resort. Descending from the Iselsberg Pass the village of **Winklern** marks the road junction where the Grossglockner road begins. Between Winklern and Heiligenblut there are five villages and three campsites. It is possible, from many centres around the mountains, to take coach trips over the Grossglocknerstrasse.

The **Grossglockner High Alpine Road** is an engineering achievement second to none. Previously there had been no

*Colourful alpine flowers on the Grossglockner*

*Heiligenblut lies in spectacular scenery*

crossing between the Brenner Pass and the Rädstadter Tauern Pass, more than 160km (100 miles) apart. The Romans used to keep the pass open all year round but this achievement has never since been equalled. Depending on the weather it is open between mid-May and mid-November but a late or early snowfall may close the road for a few days. Indeed, snow may fall at any time of year on the higher reaches, though in mid-summer it is not a problem and the road remains clear. The route used by the Romans differed slightly from that used today; when engineers were blasting to build the Hochtor Tunnel they found a Roman statuette of Hercules.

The valley of the River Möll is broad and relatively flat, rising only gently until coming to **Heiligenblut** in its dramatic setting clinging to an outcrop of rock with its church, standing out against the backdrop of the mountains, visible from a considerable distance. The town is named after its church, which was built by the monks of Admont in the fifteenth century to perpetuate prayers in the name of the relic of the Holy Blood. This relic was said to have been brought here in the tenth century by Briccius, an officer of the Court of Byzantium, whose tomb lies in the crypt. One of the greatest treasures of the church is the awe-inspiring triptych altar screen, one of the finest in Austria. In the churchyard is a 'book' with metal pages recording the names of the victims of 'our mountains'.

Heiligenblut has one of the finest mountaineering schools in Austria. In summer months it is transferred to the Kaiser Franz-Joseph Haus. Both Heiligenblut and nearby **Döllach** offer facilities for riding as well as mountaineering.

Soon after leaving Heiligenblut at 1,288m (4,225ft) the toll gate of the mountain road is reached. At an altitude of 1,913m (6,275ft) there is a viewpoint at the Kasereck offering views back to the Heiligenblut basin.

Further on there is a left fork to the **Kaiser Franz-Joseph Haus**, a large mountain hotel at an altitude of 2,418m (7,931ft). The road ends in a long terrace, mostly hewn from the rock. A short walk along this terrace provides a spectacle not to be missed. The massive glacier lying below is the Pasterze Glacier which flows for 10km (6 miles).

Beyond the hotel a path, which begins on the last platform (the Freiwandeck), leads above the glacier. It is actually a ledge on the cliff but is quite safe; the round trip takes about $1^1/_2$ hours and leads to another spectacular viewpoint. The altitude makes most people breathless so it is wise to take it easy. Also at the Freiwandeck is a funicular railway, the Gletscherbahn, allowing descent to the glacier itself. On the slope below the viewing platform numerous marmots can often be seen, and they are a popular additional attraction.

Return from the Kaiser Franz-Joseph Haus to the road fork at the Guttal, where a left turn starts the climb again. There is a viewpoint near the southern end of the Hochtor tunnel. It is as well to note that parking on the roadway is an offence so be sure to park only at designated places.

At the northern end of the tunnel is the highest point on the road at 2,505m (8,216ft). Do not worry if you car appears to be labouring — it will be caused by lack of oxygen. Nothing grows at this altitude except a few hardy mosses and even grass has disappeared far below this level. Early visitors will find themselves driving through a gorge cut in the snow. The road passes out of the East Tyrol at Hochtor to re-enter Salzburg Province.

The road now descends through the Mittertörl Tunnel at 2,261m (7,416ft) over a bare stony landscape, then ascends again to the Fuscher Törl (2,428m, 7,964ft). For part of the way the road runs along a corniche above the Seidelwinkl valley and there is an impressive view to the east.

A right fork leads up to the Edelweiss Spitze at 2,577m (8,453ft) where it is possible to park and obtain refreshments. Here there is a walk, which at this altitude requires care. The journey may be broken by a stop at the observation tower where one can sit on the  terrace and admire the breathtaking view of thirty-seven peaks over 3,000m (9,840ft) and nineteen glaciers.

The descent now starts in earnest and the views are spectacular and everchanging as the road twists and turns with twenty-six hairpin bends. After another corniche the trees reappear, followed by a ravine, and the final series of hairpin bends ends the descent to 1,145m (3,756ft) with the short run into the mountain hamlet of **Ferleiten**. **Fusch** is reached after the road crosses the river and the wooded gorge. The Bärenschlucht is negotiated on yet another, though shorter, corniche.

From Fusch to **Bruck an der Grossglocknerstrasse** is only 7km (4 miles). Bruck is in the Pinzgau valley. Better known for its association with the Grossglocknerstrasse, it is a summer and winter resort with a pleasant swimming pool, a campsite, and a famous view of Fischorn Castle nearby.

The major tourist resort in this area is **Zell am See** which is easily reached from Bruck. An excursion can be made to visit the Kaprun valley, through the gorge past the old ruined castle to the Kessel Waterfall, which is floodlit at night. A three-section cable car goes up to a height of almost 3,000m (9,840ft) to the Kitzsteinhorn where there is year-round skiing.

The town is situated where the valley broadens but beyond the town the road rises between steep mountains and ahead the wall of the Limberg Dam (Limbergsperre) suddenly looms. The Kesselfall Alpen Haus marks the limit of access for cars, but a bus shuttle service connects with the funicular to the dam. On the upward journey there are views of the valley and the dam. Above the Limberg Dam is the Mooser Dam. There is a complicated system for piping water to the power station below the dams and for pumping it back into the Wasserfallboden Lake Reservoir. The Kaprun Power Station machine rooms are open to visitors. A  pathway along the top of the first dam gives a surprising and excellent view of the water of the Wasserfallboden below and the  valley beyond. This excursion round the lakes and power station is interesting, and spectacular if the chair lift is taken. Views of the mountain ranges of Grossvenediger, the Wetterstein, the Karwendel and Kaisergebirge, and the lake at Zell-am-See can also be seen. **Kaprun** also has facilities for mountaineering, a good swimming pool and a campsite.

Further up the main valley are the typical villages of **Piesendorf** and **Walchen**. **Niedernsill** is just off the main road opposite **Steindorf**. **Lengdorf** and **Uttendorf** follow, then **Stuhlfelden** just below Mittersill. All these villages are picturesque and offer the usual facilities for visitors with cafés, restaurants, hotels and varying evening entertainments.

**Mittersill** is a winter and summer resort and is at the road junction that marks the return into the Tyrol after the most spectacular and adventurous trip round the Grossglockner High Alpine Road and the lovely peaceful valleys of the East Tyrol.

# Additional Information

## Places of Interest

**Lienz**
*Schloss Bruck and Osttiroler Heimat-
museum* (East Tyrol Museum)
Open: Easter to October 10am-5pm.

## Tourist Information Centres

**Anras**
A-9913
☎ (4846) 6595

**Bruck an der Grossglocknerstrasse**
A-5671
☎ (6545) 295, 6505

**Fusch**
A-5672
☎ (6546) 236

**Heiligenblut**
A-9844
☎ (4824) 2001-21

**Hollersbach**
A-5731
☎ (6562) 8105

**Hopfgarten in Defereggen**
A-9961
☎ (4872) 5356

**Huben**
A-9953
☎ (4872) 5238

**Innervillgraten**
A-9932
☎ (4843) 5194

**Iselsberg**
A-9991
☎ (4852) 4117

**Kals**
A-9981
☎ (4876) 211

**Kaprun**
A-5710
☎ (6547) 8643

**Kartitsch**
A-9941
☎ (4858) 5216

**Kötschach**
A-9640
☎ (4715) 8516

**Lavant**
A-9900
☎ (4852) 8216

**Lienz**
A-9900
☎ (4852) 4747

**Matrei in Osttirol**
A-9971
☎ (4875) 6527, 6709

**Mittersill**
A-5730
☎ (6562) 369

**Neukirchen am Grossvenediger**
A-5741
☎ (6565) 6256

**Niedernsill**
A-5722
☎ (6548) 8232

**Sillian**
A-9920
☎ (4842) 6280

**Stuhlfelden**
A-5724
☎ (6562) 4365

**Uttendorf**
A-5723
☎ (6563) 8279

**Winklern**
A-9841
☎ (4822) 227

**Zell am See**
A-5700
☎ (6542) 2600

# 8
# KITZBÜHEL, THE BRIXENTAL AND THE INNTAL

From Mittersill road 161 leads towards Kitzbühel, climbing to the Thurn Pass and the regional border. On the pass, which is only at 1,273m (4,175ft), there is a refreshment stop and a chance to park the car and take a stroll along the path to take in the view. To the west is the Oberpinzgau valley and due south is the Hollersbachtal, cutting deep into the Hohe Tauern.

**Jochberg** is the first village on the green slopes above Kitzbühel. A pleasant village widely spread out on the gentle slopes, it has a heated swimming pool in a delightful setting with a sunbathing lawn set amid mature trees giving a parklike appearance. There are tennis courts and 60km (37 miles) of marked paths in the splendid surrounding area.

A pleasant walk starts at the end of the forest road just south of Jochberg. There is a right turn at the Hechenmoos onto a forest road. After 4km (2 miles) take path 712. In about 30 minutes the Gruber Alm is reached after which the path goes, beyond the *alm*, to the Kelchalm Berghaus, a mountain inn at 1,432m (4,697ft). The path climbs further, past a turning to the right, and onto Karzum Tor at 1,931m (6,334ft). Descend south to the picturesque Torsee, then turn north-west to climb again to the Gamshag (2,178m, 7,144ft). The return journey passes the Schlictenalm and the Nieder-kaseralm. The path doubles back to the south before crossing the stream in the valley and returning to the starting point. Six hours should be allowed for the walk, which is of moderate difficulty.

Down the valley from Jochberg, the village of **Aurach** has two parts, lower and upper. There is a right turn towards

Oberaurach: the Auracher Graben, or trench, continues past the village. The Natur und Wildpark Aurach is a wildlife park 4km (2 miles) away along a good road. A sharp left turn on the valley road will take visitors to it. Here, red deer with splendid antlers, wild pigs, a special breed of Hungarian sheep, and many other animals, all live freely. In summer months there are occasional demonstrations with falcons and eagles. The information office in Jochberg will be able to supply opening times before a visit.

**Kitzbühel** is only about 4km (2 miles) down the valley. It is an old world town in a magnificent setting between the Kitzbüheler Alps to the south, and the Kaiser Mountains to the north. It has been a fashionable resort for many years. Long before the heyday of winter sports, visitors came because of the unmatched scenery and the warm waters of the Schwarzsee nearby.

Many people think of the town as a ski resort, which in winter it certainly is, with the famous ski run of the Hahnenhamm just to the south. Indeed, it is possible to ski 8km (5 miles) downhill, and by careful use of ski runs and lifts, there is no need to climb under one's own power. In winter the tourist has the use of fifty-six cable cars or ski lifts, sixty ski runs, cross country tracks, bobsleighs, and ice hockey facilities, together with the assistance of ski instructors. At the height of the ski season many famous faces can be seen around the town as several celebrities own chalets nearby. Other events in the winter include skating, ski races, fancy dress balls and festivals. The main roads are kept clear of snow, but the side roads are not salted to avoid 'spoiling the winter scene'.

There is plenty for the summer visitor to see and do. There is swimming in the indoor ozone pool, or lake bathing in the Schwarzsee, boating, fishing, golf, riding, bowling, or tennis on any of the twenty tennis courts. There is a lakeside campsite.

An area walking programme is available from the information office and there is even a senior citizens' walking programme suitable for a steadier pace. Also obtainable from the information office is the 'summer holiday pass' (*Sommerferienpass*) which lasts for 6 days and gives worthwhile reductions on the cable cars and chair lifts and free entry to the indoor swimming pool in the pump room.

One of the cable cars, north-west of the town, ascends in two stages to the famous Kitzbüheler Horn (1,996m, 6,547ft) with its equally famous views. It is a mountain panorama and, on clear days, one can see Chiemsee a very large lake in Germany over 48km (30 miles) away due north.

It is quite possible to walk down, following the trackway (but shortcut the bends), to the guest house Alpenhaus Kitzbüheler Horn (1,670m, 5,478ft) then on path 24 to the Pletzeralm near the middle station cable-car and the beautifully situated Adlerhutte (1,266m, 4,152ft). Here a path goes directly down, or one can walk to the guest house Hagstein (1,032m, 3,385ft) and so down to the outskirts of Kitzbühel. It is an easy walk requiring about 2 hours for the descent.

Within the town itself, which is over 1,000 years old, the main points of interest are in the old centre. The Vorderstadt and Hinterstadt are pedestrian precincts and have substantial Bavarian-style houses, often with paintings on the walls, making a very picturesque scene.

There are two churches of interest. The parish church (*Pfaffkirche*) is on a raised site and has a tall slender tower and a mountain-style overhanging roof. The triple nave is fifteenth-century Gothic. In the Chapel of St Rosa of Lima the ceiling paintings are the work of Simon-Benedikt Faistenberger (1695-1759), one of a local family of artists.

The Church of Our Lady (*Liebfrauenkirche*) is distinguished by its massive square tower which houses a sanctuary. Simon Benedikt painted the vaulting in 1739 with a picture of the Coronation of The Virgin. Reminding the visitor that the church was an important place of pilgrimage until the nineteenth century is a painting of Our Lady of Succour, Maria Hilf, which was painted in the seventeenth century.

The local museum is well worth a visit. Among the exhibits is a cross-section model of the local silver mines, in their day the deepest in the world. Part of the museum is dedicated to the early days of skiing and includes early photographs and equipment.

Evenings in Kitzbühel are, of course, well catered for. The town has a casino. The local town band performs on some evenings and there are all the usual and varied entertainments.

Only 5km (3 miles) from Kitzbühel, and in a broad green valley, is the lovely village of **Reith bei Kitzbühel**. Lying on a minor road, it is convenient for the town while offering a more peaceful environment. It is 3km (2 miles) from the Schwarzsee

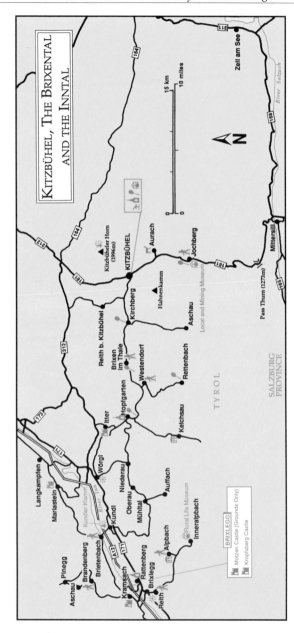

KITZBÜHEL, THE BRIXENTAL AND THE INNTAL

*The parish church and the Liebfrauenkirche, Kitzbühel*

*A quiet street and outdoor café in Kitzbühel*

and arrangements can be made in the village for fishing, boating and outings by minibus.

Road 170 passes the turning for Reith and goes up the Brixental. The first village on route is **Kirchberg**, a pleasant place with a bathing lake and a heated pool alongside. It has fifteen tennis courts among its facilities and it is on the train and bus route.

South of Kirchberg is the Spertental, with the village of **Aschau** at the end of the surfaced section of road 8km (5 miles) from the main road. The valley cuts deep into the Kitzbüheler Alps.

From the end of the unsurfaced road at the Labalm, $4^1/_2$km (3 miles) beyond Aschau, it is possible to ascend the Grosse Rettenstein, 2,362m (7,747ft). This marks the boundary between Tyrol and Salzburg and is one of the higher peaks in the range. The walk is suitable only for experienced mountain walkers.

Below Aschau, about one kilometre into the valley, is the valley station for the Gaisberg chair lift. From the mountain end of the lift the summit of Gaisberg can be easily reached in about 2 hours by paths 2 and 2a to the Bärsättalm (1,451m, 4,760ft) then path 11 to the summit at 1,767m (5,796ft). This is a good walk in a quiet pleasant valley.

Another 5km (3 miles) on up the main road is **Brixen im Thale**, which caters a little more for the tourist than Kirchberg. Here there is a splendid outdoor heated swimming pool and no less than twenty-three tennis courts with five indoor courts in the tennis hall. There is a walking programme and a free programme of guided walks, both on the hills and in the lower regions. Band concerts and the usual evening entertainments are available.

The Sennberg *Sessellift* or chairlift, goes up to Hochbrixen where there is a splendid view of the whole of the Brixental. It is possible to walk back down. There is also a tiny lake, the Erlensee, where fishing is allowed.

**Westendorf** lies just off the main road, a little higher on a plateau. It is a winter and summer resort and has an active programme of evening entertainment and band concerts on Sunday evenings. The swimming pool and sunbathing lawn are enormous and there is a programme of walks through the meadows and on the gentle hills to the south-west of the village.

There is a turning left, off the main road, into the delightful small village of **Kelchsau** where there are some interesting traditional wooden houses, some still with shingle roofs held down with large boulders — something more often seen in the more mountainous regions. At the end of the surfaced road, beyond the village, there is a fork where the valley divides. To the left is the Kurzer Grund, or Short Ground, and to the right the Langer Grund, or Long Ground. Both valleys cut deep into the Kitzbüheler Alps with the stream in the Langer Grund, the Kelchsauer Ache, rising high up near the Kreuzjoch at 2,558m (8,390ft) which is more than 15km (9 miles) from the fork. The river is used by white water canoeists.

The turning into the Kelchsauer valley is almost at the outskirts of **Hopfgarten**, a stately market town in beautiful surroundings. Hopfgarten prides itself on the profusion of flowers in the town and, though of modest size, there is evening entertainment in the two modern cafés and in other establishments. Riding, tennis and mini-golf are available, as is a swimming pool. In the centre of the town is the twin-towered parish church of St Jakob and St Leonhard, known as the 'Proud Cathedral of the Farmers'.

Near the foot of the chair lift there is a car park. The chair lift goes up to the Hohe Salve in three stages from 621m (2,037ft) in the valley, 1,156m (3,792ft) at the first station, 1,532m (5,025ft) at the second station where there are excellent views, to 1,827m (5,993ft) at the top. Refreshments are available near all three stations. The views from the summit are even better than the excellent views lower down, as each widens to include the more distant snowcapped peaks.

Just off the main road is a tiny hamlet with a history going back 1,000 years. Dating from AD902, **Itter** was originally in the Regensburg See but in 1380 came into the care of the Archbishop of Salzburg. Today the castle is a luxury hotel, restored to some extent. Leading towards it, the street is lined with guest houses and pensions and there is a nearby campsite. In the surrounding meadows there is a network of footpaths and also a swimming pool nearby. A descent of 180m (590ft) in 8km (5 miles) to **Wörgl** and the Inn valley is reached once again. Wörgl is a thriving small market town well situated in the Inn valley, with a nearby motorway and main railway line. It is a convenient centre for touring the surrounding areas.

Within the town, or nearby, are all the usual facilities for evening entertainment including band concerts. Daytime activities include riding and cycling. Not only is there a programme of guided walks but also guided cycle rides. Information concerning galleries and exhibitions of various sorts in the town can be obtained from the information office.

South-east from the town centre a minor road leads to one of those quiet, tucked-away valleys which are such a delightful part of this country. This is the Wildeschönau, a wonderfully romantic valley with three small villages. In order of approach from Wörgl they are **Niederau, Oberau** and **Auffach**. Between them they offer a surprising number of facilities, including a mountain rural life museum which is very interesting. Near Niederau there is a small bathing lake and two chair lifts bringing the green wooded higher slopes within easier reach.

Anyone using the campsite between Wörgl and **Kundl** (it is alongside road 171), can take a circular walk and visit a romantic gorge. From the campsite go south-west to the guest house Köfler, uphill to the guest house Zuaberwinkl, then on mostly level ground to the village of Oberau. Go south-west to Muhlthal then north-west, gently downhill, alongside the river. After about 2km (1 mile) the valley narrows into the Kundler Klamm or gorge. Near the bottom of the gorge is the guest house Klamm, with a ruined castle just below. The road is rejoined near Kundl. A footpath goes back towards the campsite just on the edge of the woods south of the road. The walk uses very good paths in delightful scenery. The distance is about 16km (10 miles) which is a good day's outing at a gentle pace.

One of Europe's gems is **Rattenberg**, once a rich and famous mining town like its neighbour Schwaz. However, its mining period was comparatively short. Between 1500 and 1560 2,000 tons of silver were extracted. The town is near a narrow section of the River Inn and by exerting control over river traffic the town was saved. The unfortunate collapse of the mining industry meant that the town was quite poor and so missed the building of the Baroque era. Today, it is an unspoilt medieval town and the smallest in Austria.

There are the ruins of a castle in the town, which may be visited. From the terrace at the foot of the tower there is an excellent view over the town. *Schlossbergspiele* (concerts in the castle) are held here occasionally.

The parish church, alongside the bluff on which the castle stands, is well worth a visit. It was constructed in 1473 in Gothic style, using blocks of pink marble. Inside, the two naves are of differing lengths: the shorter and most southerly has stalls against a windowless wall 'for the miners'. Most of the wall paintings are attributed to Matthäus Günter who also painted the pictures in the parish church at Wilten. His painting here of the Last Supper is worthy of note.

The High Street, where the medieval houses have plain façades decorated with window and door frames in pink marble, is very interesting. Along with its neighbour across the river, Rattenberg is famous for engraved and finely modelled glassware, and many of its shops hold glittering displays of exquisite work.

**Brixlegg** is only a very short distance south and is the gateway to the Alpbachtal, a superlative valley. The way into the valley is by way of Reith; however, Brixlegg itself has some interesting places to visit. Matzen Castle lies in the middle of natural parklike surroundings; it dates from 1176 and is well worth seeing. Almost at the entrance to the Zillertal is the ruined Kropfsberg Castle, which was built to defend it. It is a most splendid ruin and worthy of a visit.

Between these two, which are a little over 2km (1 mile) apart, are the castles of Lichtenwerth and Lipperheide which are on either side of the road.

Brixlegg is something of a spa and has a hot mineral bath, Minerlbad Mehrn, where it is claimed the calcium sulphate waters cure diverse complaints. The parish church of Our Lady is worth visiting. Tennis courts are available in Matzenpark and there is also an open air swimming pool and fishing can be arranged. Evening entertainment follows the usual pattern with band concerts on some evenings.

**Reith** is quite small but is welcoming to tourists. Voted by an international jury in Brussels 'the best flower decorated village in Europe', the residents obviously work hard to maintain the good appearance of the village. In the middle of the village is a small lake, the Reither See, where bathing is allowed. A chair lift enables visitors to easily visit the Reither Kogel at 1,337m (4,385ft), where there are fantastic views both up and down the Inn valley and up the Zillertal. There are facilities for fishing and tennis and pathways for gentle strolling or hard walking, whichever one chooses.

Evening entertainment in the village follows the usual course, but there is also a *bauern theater*, a farmers' theatre or folk group, performed in traditional manner and often in dialect. This provides an unusual and entertaining evening, even if one is at a disadvantage with the language.

Higher up the valley, the villages of **Alpbach** and **Inneralpbach** are fine examples of alpine villages. Most of the houses are beautiful specimens of the art of building in wood. Coming up the valley, the guest house Achenwirt is below Alpbach and about 5km (3 miles) from Reith. Here is the start of the two-section chair lift, going up to 1,804m (5,917ft) and making light work of the summit of the Wiedersberge Horn at 2,127m (6,976ft). From here there is another spectacular viewpoint, a panorama taking in the Zillertal, the Stubai Glaciers, the Karwendel, and Kaiser Mountains. For the energetic there is a choice of paths back down, with refreshments halfway at the Almhof.

At Lagerhause there is a sharp left turn and a short climb to Alpbach, while Inneralpbach is straight on. There is an information office providing details of a programme of walks, an indoor swimming pool, tennis courts, evening concerts and slide shows. At Inneralpbach is a Rural Life Museum which is very interesting. The valley is a winter as well as summer resort and is possibly busier in winter when eighteen ski lifts are in operation.

Back in the main valley, cross the River Inn at Brixlegg for **Kramsach**, which has a reputation for its fine glass works. In the town there is a school teaching the art of painting, etching and engraving glass. Near the town is the seventeenth-century Castle Achenrain and five small lakes. There is a sixth lake higher up beyond Mosen, the Berglsteiner See. The larger of the lower ones is the Reintaler See, while next is the Krumm See. All three have bathing facilities and adjacent guest houses named after the lakes. The lakes are on a plateau 100m (328ft) above the River Inn.

There is a campsite down by the river near its junction with the Brandenberger Ache. This flows down the valley past the village of **Brandenberg**. The river actually rises in Germany from two different sources and its confluence is in Austria, a few kilometres north. It flows down through some of the beautiful wooded valleys of the Brandenberger Alps.

An easy walk of some 8km (5 miles) can be taken down the lower reaches of the Brandenberg valley. Take the bus to Brandenberg near the church, then take the path to the river.

First, however, it is worth taking a stroll round the village in its beautiful setting surrounded by woods. Cross the river bridge to the west bank and walk downstream through the Trefenbach Klamm on a good path, then a track. This track crosses the river again just outside Kramsach at the hamlet of Mariathal.

At this point, but on the west bank, is the valley station of the Rosskogel lift, otherwise known as the Sonnwendjoch Berg Bahn. The lift goes up in two stages to 1,790m (5,871ft) near the Rosskogel Hut, where many visitors go for the higher level walking over a grassy plateau and then down to the Zireiner See, on a good, wide and safe path. Here is an alpine jewel, a lake set in a grassy hollow with paths round about. It marks the eastern limit of the Rofan Mountains which the Achensee guards at the western end.

Kramsach boasts 60km (37 miles) of low level paths and 90km (56 miles) of mountain path. Temperatures in the Zireinsee will be lower due to the altitude, but the lower lakes near the village have a summer average temperature of 22° to 26°C (72 to 79°F).

The opportunity to visit the open air museum of Tyrolean farm buildings, the Freilichtmuseum Tiroler Bauernhof, should not be missed. Here many typical wooden houses and farm buildings are preserved in a pleasant lakeside meadowland. They have been carefully rebuilt and are widely spaced for the best effect. They give a unique insight into the way of life of generations of mountain farmers.

By far the prettiest route northwards is the old road from Kramsach, past the lakes, on the northern bank of the Inn to the small village of **Breitenbach am Inn**. The motorway, the main road, and the railway are all on the other side of the river thus leaving this village in peace. It has a swimming pool and a network of footpaths for gentle walks, and evening entertainments for most tastes from band concerts to folk singers.

Still on the north bank of the river, 8km (5 miles) from Breitenbach, there is a fork in the road. The right fork takes the road back across the river to Kirchbichl and Bad Häring. *Bad* means 'bath' or 'spa' and there is a pump room, or *Kurhaus*, though not on a grand scale.

The left fork goes over a ridge into a quiet valley and to the tiny hamlet of **Mariastein**. The attraction which for many years has drawn pilgrims, visitors and tourists, is the castle. When the massive tower was built in the fourteenth century, it was for the purpose of defence. However, the Lady Chapel became a place of pilgrimage and gradually this aspect became more important. From the castle courtyard, stairs lead to the Rittersaal, or Knights' Hall, which contains the treasures of the castle, the crown and sceptre of the Counts of the Tyrol. Opening times can be obtained from the tourist information centre.

On the upper floors are two chapels. The lower one is the Kreuzkapelle or Chapel of the Cross and this has a Gothic interior dating from the sixteenth century. The upper Chapel of Miracles, Gnadenkapelle, was redecorated in the nineteenth century when it was restored to the original Baroque. At the same time the windows were enlarged, thus improving the lighting. The statue of the Virgin dates from the fifteenth century.

Continuing northwards, Schloss Schömwörth is just outside **Nieder Breitenbach**. This and the next village of **Unter Lang-kampfen** are all within 5km (3 miles) of each other and the latter is only 8km (5 miles) from the centre of Kufstein.

## Additional Information

### Places of Interest

**Aurach**
*Natur und Wildpark Aurach*
6km (4 miles) south of Kitzbühel on road 161, then through Oberaurach, 4km (3 miles) up the valley. Bus service.
Open: daily 9am-5pm.

**Inneralpbach**
*Rural Life Museum*
Open: daily except Tuesdays, 10am-12noon and 1-5pm.

**Jochberg**
*Local and Mining Museum*
Open: Tuesday and Thursday 5-7pm, Sunday 10am-12noon.

**Kitzbühel**
*Heimatmuseum*
Near town centre
Open: 9am-12noon. Closed Sundays and holidays.

### Tourist Information Centres

**Alpbach**
A-6236
☎ (5336) 5211

**Aurach**
A-6370
☎ (5356) 4622

**Brandenberg**
A-6234
☎ (5331) 5203

**Breitenbach am Inn**
A-6250
☎ (5338) 7738

**Brixen im Thale**
A-6364
☎ (5334) 8111

**Brixlegg**
A-6230
☎ (5337) 2581

**Hopfgarten**
A-6361
☎ (5335) 2322

**Itter**
A-6300
☎ (5335) 2670

**Jochberg**
A-6373
☎ (5355) 5229

**Kelchsau**
A-6361
☎ (5335) 8105

**Kirchberg**
A-2880
☎ (2641) 2226, 2460

**Kitzbühel**
A-6370
☎ (5356) 2272, 2155

**Kramsach**
A-6233
☎ (5337) 2209, 2710

**Kundl**
A-6250
☎ (5338) 7326, 8312

**Mariastein**
A-6322
☎ (5332) 6485

**Reith**
A-6370
☎ (5356) 5465

**Westendorf**
A-6363
☎ (5334) 6230, 6550

**Wörgl**
A-6300
☎ (5332) 2122

# 9
# KUFSTEIN AND THE KAISER MOUNTAINS

The medieval fortified town of **Kufstein** on the River Inn is dominated by its massive fortress, or *Festung*. The town lies at the centre of a delightful part of the country where mountain walking is made easier by the network of good paths penetrating the valley and ascending the peaks of the Kaiser Gebirge. There are warm lakes for bathing not far from the town, as well as romantic woods and flower-decked meadows.

To the east it is possible to make a circuit round the area known as the Ferienwinkel am Kaiser, or 'holiday corner on the Kaiser', which is a beautiful area of wooded valleys, quiet villages, lakes and rivers.

As it is only about 2 hours from Munich by motorway, the area is popular with the Bavarians, but is little known to British visitors who tend to go to the Zillertal, Salzburg or Zell-am-See. Bordered on the east by the Loferer and Leoganger Steinberg range, which form the border with Salzburg Province, on the north by Germany, and on the east by the gentle Brandenberger Alps, it is an excellent area for a winter or summer visit.

The Kaiser Gebirge, or Emperor Mountains, are really two ranges, with the Wilder (or wild) Kaiser to the south rising to 2,344m (7,688ft), and the smaller northern range, the Zahmer (or gentle) Kaiser rising to 1,997m (6,550ft).

Geroldseck Festung was built by the Dukes of Bavaria in the twelfth century to guard the entrance to the Inn valley. When the fortress commander was under siege by a Bavarian force in 1703 he had the town burnt to give him a clear line of fire. The fortress has withstood many sieges and on show are some of the guns and cannon used. Later it was used as a political prison and the cells may be seen with mementoes of some of its famous prisoners. It is now the town museum and English speaking guides are available.  The Emperor's Tower is the larger, higher tower with walls $4^1/_2$m (15ft) thick and built round a central column. It is encircled by a vaulted gallery. On one level are the guns and on a higher level the cells of the political prisoners. A deep well over 68m (223ft) deep was bored in the rock and there is an ingenious way of raising the water using a treadmill.

Also part of the fortress, in the Burghers' Tower, is the Heldenorgel, or Heroes Organ, which is controlled from the gallery for the audience at the foot of the rock. It is claimed that on a still day the organ can be heard from a distance of 8km (5 miles). It was first played in 1931 having been built as a memorial to the Austrian and German dead of World War I. Daily recitals are given at noon.

An approach to the fortress can be made from near the church in the Unterer Stadtplatz, where a covered stairway goes beneath the Burghers' Tower. An easier, but much less interesting, approach is by lift from the riverside promenade. Following a tour of the museum, which includes the Emperor's Tower, it is possible to stroll around the outer walls, and explore the many storage rooms. There are splendid views of the district across the river to  Pendling, 1,563m (5,127ft) or east to the Kaiser Mountains.

Kufstein has a smart shopping centre spreading out from the Oberer Stadtplatz, and a romantic old street below the fortress, the Römerhofgasse, which contains the oldest winehouse in the Tyrol, the Batzenhäusl. There are free guided tours of the town which take in the Heldenhügel, or Hero's Hill, where there is a statue of Andreas Hofer who fought the French and Bavarians here in 1809. From the bluff there is a good view of the position of the fortress.

In addition to four bathing lakes there is a swimming pool, tennis, fishing, numerous footpaths, and four chair lifts. The chair lifts make possible an easy approach to the Kaiser Mountains though most of the peaks are only for experienced mountain walkers. Paths on the lower slopes are good and a local sketch map can be obtained from the tourist information office.

An idyllic tour west of Kufstein takes in some of the most beautiful lake scenery in the Tyrol. A bus service from Kufstein

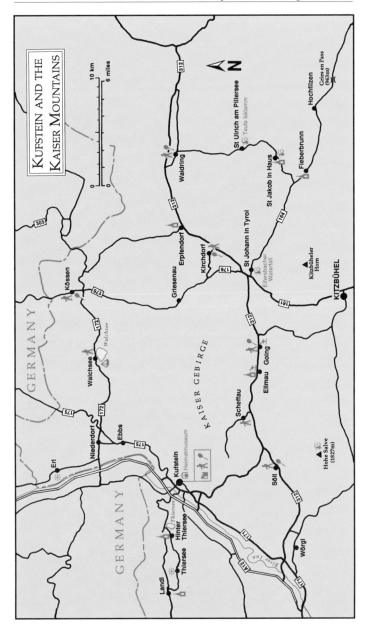

KUFSTEIN AND THE
KAISER MOUNTAINS

10 km
6 miles

N

GERMANY

GERMANY

KAISER GEBIRGE

312

312

305

172

175

176

312

312

164

161

176

175

171

417

171

Walchsee

Thiersee

Brixentaler

Kitzbüheler
Horn

Hohe Salve
(1827m)

Gries en Pass
(965m)

Hochfilzen

St Ulrich am Pillersee
Teufe Isklamm

Fieberbrunn

St Jakob In Haus

St Johann In Tyrol
Eifersbacher
Waterfall

KITZBÜHEL

Waldring

Erpfendorf

Kirchdorf

Griesenau

Kössen

Walchsee

Niederdorf

Ebbs

Erl

Landl

Hinter
Thiersee

Thiersee

Kufstein
Heimatmuseum

Scheffau

Ellmau

Going

Söll

Wörgl

*Kufstein fortress*

*A rooftop view of Kufstein*

runs to Hecht See — a beautiful lake with splendid facilities for bathing and refreshments. A footpath goes all the way round the lake, just on the edge of the woods which enclose the lake and its sunbathing meadow. The walk can be extended to take in the Egel See or the Läng See which are smaller lakes, without facilities, nearby. The ruined Thierberg Castle is near Läng See.

The hamlets of Vorder Thiersee, Hinter Thiersee and Landl are situated in this pleasant green valley. Between them the villages boast three indoor pools, or *Hallenbad*, 200km (124 miles) of footpaths, three tennis courts, band concerts, and a folk theatre. Furthest from Kufstein is **Landl**, a scattering of pleasant modern houses with a traditional church, a swimming pool, bowling alley and the smart Gasthof Zum Post. **Hinter Thiersee** lies higher and a little off the main road. A pleasant village in broad meadows below the woodland, its church has a straight spire instead of the more familiar onion-shaped dome. **Thiersee**, village and lake, has boating and fishing facilities as well as lake bathing. A campsite is close by the lake shore and there are many facilities for refreshments.

Thiersee is also known for its passion play. The play, which began in the seventeenth century, has been re-enacted every 6 years, interrupted only by World War II, and was last performed in 1988. A newly built theatre which seats 900 is now its home. It is performed by a village amateur group and non-villagers are not allowed to take part.

To take a tour round the Kaiser Gebirge, leave Kufstein by the road south, number 173, which is partly in a pretty rocky gorge, although spoilt by quarrying in a few places. Local folk tales tell of many spirits abroad in this region. Charlemagne supposedly lies buried beneath the Wilder Kaiser; in a cave there is a sleeping prince guarded by seven giants; beneath one of the peaks, the Totenkirchl, there is a female giant. However, such tales are difficult to envisage in the peace and tranquillity of the high pathways.

Where road 173 meets the main road, 312, turn right for **Söll** which is only 2km (1 mile) from the junction. The main part of the village lies back from the main road. A chair lift goes up to the Hohe Salve at 1,827m (5,993ft). Altogether there are 120km (75 miles) of marked and cleared footpaths, with 500 seats. Splendid views of the southern aspect of the Wilder Kaiser, which shows very light-coloured in the sunshine, may be obtained from the village and surroundings. All the usual facilities, including a guided tour of a farm, and evening entertainment are available and the Moorsee is a delightful small lake easily reached from the village.

The next village on the tour is reached by turning north off road 312 on a minor road to **Scheffau**. Lying well back off the main road, and being on a no-through road backing onto the mountains, this is a very quiet village and lays claim to having particularly pure air. The village is a good centre for walking, lying as it does at the centre of a network of paths. There is a swimming pool, or one can go up to the Hintersteiner See. A most peaceful and easy walk is round the lake, the southern shore of which is tree lined. A forest road goes along the north bank to a swimming place and beyond to the guest house Widauer, which is the point from which to start the return journey. It is an easy walk of about 2 hours.

The next two villages, Ellmau and Going, again just off the main road, are typically Tyrolean. **Ellmau** has wooden fronted houses on the main street and a charming little chapel. **Going** has a beautiful bathing lake, a walking programme and facilities for tennis, bowling and squash. All these villages, of course, have facilities for winter sports.

In the next few kilometres the road leads to **St Johann in Tyrol**, largest town in the area, a market town and holiday centre for this corner of Austria. Second only to Kitzbühel as a winter sports centre, it provides facilities of equal quality but, being less fashionable, is less expensive. To be fair to the rest of the Tyrol, every town and village has facilities which would more than satisfy the average visitor's needs.

The other famous skiing hill, the Kitzbüheler Horn can be reached easily from St Johann. Cable cars go up to the Anger Alm at 1,295m (4,248ft) and on up to the Harschbichl at 1,604m (5,261ft). This is on a lower northern promontory from the summit proper; a saddle, slightly lower, must first be crossed if the summit of the Kitzbüheler Horn itself, at 1,998m (6,553ft) is to be gained.

St Johann has splendid facilities for swimming, indoors and out, but the surrounding lakes may be reached in about 20 minutes by car and most are on or near the bus routes.

*The Kaisergebirge from
St Johann*

*Eifersbacher Waterfall,
St Johann*

*The interior of the church at St Johann*

*The annual ceremony of 'Bringing down the cows', St Johann*

The town lies in a large flat area at the junction of two valleys, thus, as a centre, it has the best of all worlds. Kitzbühel can be reached in 20 minutes, Kufstein in an hour, the surrounding mountains in decidedly less, while a day trip to Salzburg or to Chiemsee in Bavaria are also possible. It has a climbing school and a school for ramblers: mountain walking needs some expertise, though the town claims 100km (62 miles) of promenades and gentle paths and, being in such a large open space, it is possible, maybe uniquely so for the Tyrol, to walk a surprisingly long way on level ground.

 A recommended interesting and varied walk which takes about 3 hours is to visit the Eifersbacher Waterfall. From the new churchyard on Fieberbrunner road (just past where the road goes under the railway) go up Mag Ed Angerer Weg. Then follow the signs to the waterfall, passing a chapel and mineral spring at Theresianbad, once noted for curing rheumatism. After the waterfall return along a track via Grander-Schupf. The path is easy, except where it climbs steeply past the waterfall.

Not being content with one summer dry toboggan run, or *Sommerrodelbahn*, St Johann has a double one. Little toboggans on wheels run down a half-section concrete runway. The only control is a brake and steering is effected by the shape of the runway. A chair lift takes the customer to the top of the run where they are launched.

The town has guided walks and a special programme matched to the steadier pace of senior citizens. As a tourist centre it has an active evening entertainment programme. There is nothing more pleasant after a day walking in the mountains than to relax on a terrace with a drink and to listen to the town band in concert from the open-air pavilion.

In September there is a festival with a rather special event. On the Saturday afternoon, in the Speckbacher Strasse a long table is set down the centre of the street for the Dumpling Feast when dumplings are consumed in great quantity.

Should the visitor desire a less bustling centre from which to explore the surrounding area, then 5km (3 miles) to the north, on road 312, is **Kirchdorf**. The main part of the village lies off the main road in a broad valley with a glorious view of the east face of the Wilder Kaiser. Facilities for many sports can be found in and around the village and they operate a walking programme.

One of the walks must be to the Nieder Kaiser whether one starts from Kirchdorf or St Johann. This ridge extends far to the east of the main group and at its highest point is only 1,279m (4,195ft) high, mostly wooded, with a steep craggy slope to the south. At the eastern end, near the fork in the path which leads to the main ridge, is the Gmailkapelle and close by the Lourdes Grotte, site of some miraculous cures many years ago.

To continue the tour, go south-east from St Johann towards Pass Griessen (963m, 3,159ft), also called the Hochfilzen Pass after the village of the same name. It was near here, not many years ago, that during an army exercise, when the group 'guarding' the border were being driven back by the group 'invading' from Salzburg Province, the proud traditions of the Tyrol were upheld. Much to the amazement of a visiting observer, the locals turned out in force with pitchforks, scythes and shotguns to join in repelling the 'invaders'.

Between St Johann and the pass there are three villages, Fieberbrunn, Fiestenau and Hochfilzen. There is little to choose between them. All are pretty, and though some claim **Fieberbrunn** to be the prettiest, with its beautiful church interior and small St Jacob's chapel, it is a matter of opinion. The chapel, like many others in the Tyrol is now a memorial to those who died in the two World Wars. All of them have facilities for winter and summer holidaymakers in this splendid quiet corner of the Tyrol.

Fieberbrunn has some history as a spa where people came to 'take the waters'. In fact the name translates as 'Fever Spring'. Swimming is available at the small lake known as Lauchsee, in the heated outdoor pool, or indoors in the village.

There is a minor road going from Hochfilzen to **Flecken** or it is possible to reach Flecken by returning past the right turn to **St Jakob in Haus** and so to Flecken. Just a little way along the road north is **St Ulrich am Pillersee**.

Its own claim to be 'an island of quiet' is correct. The only reason to travel on this quiet road is to reach one of these three hamlets. St Ulrich is another gem, with its church predominant against a backdrop of green hills. The lake is quite large, about 2km (1 mile) long, and has facilities for boating, windsailing and fishing.

Apart from the facilities for high level walking in the Steinberge Mountains, the area has a large number of level marked paths around the village. A favourite walk is round the lake, taking about 3 hours. The opportunity should be taken on this walk to visit the Kapelle St Adolari dating from 1013, and also the Teufelsklamm or Devil's Gorge, where there is a lovely waterfall.

Should there be an odd wet day, there is a bowling alley and an indoor pool. St Ulrich also boasts a cure bath for asthma and neuralgic complaints. Every guest attending the greeting ceremony for the incoming visitors, *Begrussungsabend*, gets a free drink, the rather potent obstler which is akin to schnapps.

North of Pillersee the road goes through a deep wooded gorge for a short stretch until, at the head of the valley, where the minor road meets the main 312 Salzburg to St Johann road, is **Waidring**, a picturesque hamlet grouped around a central square with a fountain. Some of the houses still have roofs of shingles held down by large stones and, of course, the balconies are flower decked.

Walking in the lovely woods and meadows is delightful and the village claims 53km (33 miles) of footpaths. There is a programme of guided walks and the more adventurous, or hardy,

*The brass band in local costume at Fieberbrunn*

may ascend the Steinplatte, 1,869m (6,130ft) which is due north of the village and on the border of Salzburg Province. The walk is moderate and requires 3 hours. The walking route, *Durchkaser*, is an alpine path selected as a path for novice alpinists; the information office will supply details.

There is a wood carving school in the village preserving one of the traditions of the Tyrol. Facilities include a heated swimming pool, tennis courts and a bowling alley. There are band concerts on some evenings.

Heading west on the main road (sign-posted to St Johann) for 8km (5 miles) past Waidring, there is a road junction and the village of **Erpfendorf**. This small village, fortunate enough to be by-passed by the main road, is unremarkable on the whole in this land where most villages are so picturesque. However, students of architecture will want to see the modern church which is the work of Clemens Holzmeister, an Austrian master of contemporary religious architecture. The stained glass windows were finished in 1971 and other recent work includes mosaics in the chancel and a wooden rood beam showing the Crucifixion.

At this point St Johann is only 8km (5 miles) south. To the north is the Kössener Tal which appropriately ends at Kössen. This is a pleasant drive of about 18km (11 miles) along a good road which descends gently with the mighty river, here called the Grosse Ache though when it crosses the border into Germany it becomes the Tiroler Ache.

**Kössen**, with three other hamlets, is situated on a large, mostly level, area at a junction of two valleys. It is a delightful spot to use as a centre, for a few days or for an entire holiday.

To the south is a chair lift going up in two sections to 1,690m (5,543ft). A path continues south to the summit of the Unterberg Horn at 1,773m (5,815ft). A longer walk can be taken by heading south from the summit to the Lack-Alm (1,312m, 4,303ft). There is a sharp right turn, and a descent down the side of the Niederhauser Tal. Cross the stream of the same name and follow it downstream to the guest house Kucknerhof. There is a right fork. The walk is 10km (6 miles) long, nearly all downhill on good paths, and takes about 3 hours from the top of the chair lift.

To the north of the village the river passes through a wooded gorge. A modern metal bridge carries a pathway across the river creating a splendid vantage point. The villages provide all the usual sports — there is even a hang-gliding school — and evening entertainments include a folk theatre, band concerts and Tyrolean evenings.

**Walchsee** is a little way to the west, where the lake and village share the name. As one might expect with a warm water lake, it is extensively equipped for water sports from bathing to waterskiing, boating to windsurfing. There is a windsurfing school and an extensive network of footpaths around the area. It is possible to walk all round the lake and there is an excellent view of the village from across the water.

The circuit of the Kaiser Mountains is now almost complete and the hamlet of Durchholzen marks the start of the descent back to the Inn valley. The road forks 6km (4 miles) past Durchholzen. To the left (southerly) are the villages of **Ebbs** and **Oberndorf**, both with good facilities for visitors. The right fork goes to **Niederndorf** and Erl. All four villages are in the main Inn valley in most beautiful surroundings of broad green meadows with the mountains in the background.

The village of **Erl** must have special mention as it is home to one of the oldest passion plays of the alpine regions, with origins which can be traced back to 1613. Not so internationally-known as Oberammergau, the audiences tend to be largely Austrian and Bavarian, though recent performances have attracted over 100,000 visitors. Produced every 6 years, it will be performed in 1991, 1997, etc. In 1958 a new theatre, seating 1,500 people, was built on the edge of the village. It has a varied programme including folk music, orchestral concerts, and the world famous Vienna Boys Choir.

Having entered the Tyrol over the high pass from the Vorarlberg the tour is now complete.

# Additional Information

## Places of Interest

**Kufstein**
*Heimatmuseum*
Housed in fortress
Open: April to October daily
except Mondays, 9am-6pm. Tours
in English, taking $1^{1}/_{4}$ hours, start
9.30am, 11am, 1.45pm, 3.15pm and
4.45pm.

## Tourist Information Centres

**Aschau**
A-6274
☎ (5282) 2923

**Ebbs**
A-6341
☎ (5373) 2326

**Ellmau**
A-6352
☎ (5358) 2301, 2050

**Erl**
A-6343
☎ (5373) 8117

**Erpfendorf**
A-6383
☎ (5352) 8150

**Fieberbrunn**
A-6391
☎ (5354) 6304, 6305

**Going**
A-6353
☎ (5358) 2438

**Hinter Thiersee**
A-6335
☎ (5376) 5597

**Kirchdorf**
A-6382
☎ (5352) 3136, 3995

**Kössen**
A-6345
☎ (5375) 6287

**Kufstein**
A-6330
☎ (5372) 2207

**Landl**
A-6335
☎ (5376) 5880

**Niederndorf**
A-6342
☎ (5373) 61377

**Oberndorf**
A-6372
☎ (5352) 2927

**St Jakob in Haus**
A-6391
☎ (5354) 88159

**St Johann in Tyrol**
A-6380
☎ (5352) 2218, 3335

**St Ulrich am Pillersee**
A-6393
☎ (5354) 88192

**Scheffau**
A-6351
☎ (5358) 8137

**Söll**
A-6306
☎ (5333) 5216

**Thiersee**
A-6335
☎ (5376) 5230

**Waidring**
A-6384
☎ (5353) 5242

**Walchsee**
A-6344
☎ (5374) 5223, 5775

# *Austria Fact File*

## *Accommodation*

### Apartments

In many villages apartments are available for rental. These are almost always clean, well equipped, and relatively inexpensive. They make an ideal base from which to tour, particularly for families, and are often available at short notice without prior booking. Tourist offices will have details of their locality.

### Camping and Caravanning

No customs documents (carnet) are required for caravan trailers entering Austria. Motorists with caravans are advised tochwith their automobile club about any given route as many passes are not recommended for, or are closed to, caravans. Austria has an extensive network of camping facilities. At most sites reductions are granted to children as well as to members of FICC, AIT and FIA. The usual international rates are charged for the parking of vehicles and trailers. It is possible to camp outside these sites, provided permission has been obtained beforehand from the landowner.

Except in Vienna and in protected rural areas visitors are permitted to sleep in camping vehicles outside camping sites. But local restrictions can apply, and campers are not allowed to set up camping equipment beside their vehicle.

A list of the camping sites is available at all branches of the Austrian National Tourist Office, at Austrian Automobile Clubs and at the Austrian Camping Club.

### Farmhouses

These are economical for families, picturesque and very pleasant. Most offer bed and breakfast only. The Austrian National Tourist Office will provide a list.

### Gasthof
German for country hotel, of moderate size with a good restaurant, often indistinguishable from a hotel.

### Gasthaus
A country inn. Often the emphasis is on food and drink, but most have beds. Pensions are often called a Frühstücks-Pensions. These are guest houses offering bed and breakfast only.

### Hotels
This is the most expensive and most luxurious way to stay. It is advisable to make inquiries and reservations well in advance (especially for July, August, Christmas and Easter). Room reservations are binding for the hotel-keeper and for the guest or travel agency. Compensation may be claimed if reserved rooms are not occupied.

### Youth Hostels
Youth hostels exist in many places in Austria. They are available for young people who carry a membership card of the International Youth Hostel Association. The *International Youth Hostels Guide to Budget Accommodation* lists information and facts for each hostel in Austria. Information is in English, French, German and Spanish.

It is advisable to book in advance. More details are contained in lists available at the Austrian National Tourist Office and by the Österreichischer Jugendherbergs-verband
Schottenring 28
A-1010 Vienna
☎ 1/533 53 53

### Zimmer (Bed and Breakfast)
A great many private houses erect a sign *Zimmer* (room) and offer the service of a cheap, clean, comfortable room (often with en-suite facilities) together with a breakfast of rolls and coffee. There is almost certain to be at least one in even the smallest village.

## Arrival and Customs

Applications for an Austrian entry visa should send the completed and signed application form(s), together with a valid national passport and the fee to the appropriate Austrian Consulate (see list of embassies and consulates). For transit through Austria the visa from the neighbouring country which will be entered after leaving Austria should be obtained first.

Nationals of most European and many overseas countries need no visa to enter Austria, only a valid passport expired within less than 5 years is sufficient. Foreign nationals need no customs documents for their own cars when driving into Austria. Recognition is accorded to most driving licences and registration documents issued in other countries. Motor vehicles must be covered by third-party insurance. Motorists from some countries are required to have a Green Card as proof of third-party insurance. Information may be obtained from all automobile clubs.

Dogs and cats are allowed into Austria if their owners produce a valid vaccination certificate against rabies with an officially certified German translation. All personal belongings needed for a visit are duty free.

## Banks

Usually open 8am-12.30pm and 1.30-3pm on Monday, Tuesday, Wednesday and Friday; from 8am-12.30pm and 1.30-5.30pm on Thursday; banks are closed on Saturdays and Sundays. The exchange counters at airports and main railway stations are usually open from the first to the last plane or train, ie from 8am-10pm, 7 days a week.

## Chemists

All towns and villages have doctors and chemists. Chemists' shops (*Apotheken*) operate a rota system for night and Sunday duty; when closed a notice is displayed giving the addresses of the nearest chemists that are open. Information about the medical emergency service (*Ärztenotdienst*) is obtainable from the local police station as well as from the telephone directory. All mountain resorts have a mountain rescue service (*Bergrettungsdienst*).

## Climate and Clothing

Austria has a moderate Central European climate. However, temperatures vary according to altitude and geographical loca-

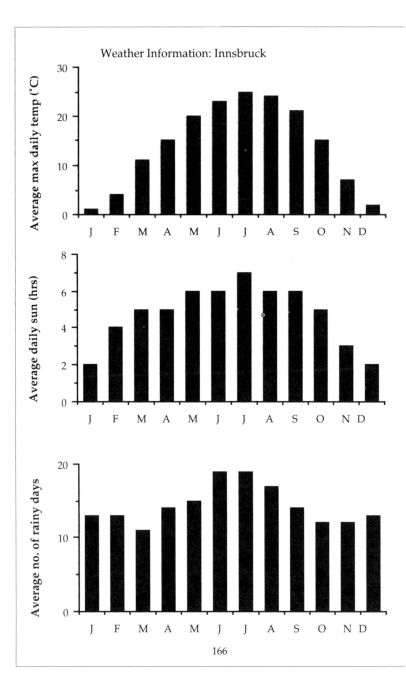

Weather Information: Innsbruck

tion. For walking in the mountains good boots and proper protection against the weather is essential. In spring and autumn a topcoat, sweater, or jacket, is advisable and, although summer days are hot, the evenings, especially in mountain resorts, can be cool. July and August are the warmest months, December and January the coldest.

## Credit Cards

The credit cards you will find most useful in Austria are American Express, Diners Club and Visa. However, outside major cities credit cards are rarely accepted.

## Currency and Exchange

The unit of currency is the Austrian Schilling, which is divided into 100 Groschen. There are bank notes to the value of 5,000, 1,000, 500, 100, 50 and 20 Schillings, coins to the value of 500, 100, 50, 25, 20, 10, 5 and 1 Schillings and fractional currency to the value of 50, 10, 5 and 2 Groschen. Foreign currency, traveller's cheques, etc may be changed into Austrian Schillings at all banks at the official rate fixed by the Vienna Stock Exchange. Currency exchange offices at railway stations and airports charge an additional 'handling fee'. Most travel agencies and hotels also have facilities for changing money. Currencies not listed on the Vienna Stock Exchange are traded at free market rates. Austrian currency may be brought in in unlimited quantities, but only a total of 100,000 Schillings may be taken out without special permission.

## Electricity

Austria uses 220 volts AC at 50 cycles/second. The plugs used are two-pin round. Some hotels stock adaptor plugs.

## Embassies and Consulates

**Australia**
12 Talbot Street,
Forrest ACT 2603
Canberra
☎ (06) 295 13 76 or 295 15 33

30 Argyle Street
Breakfast Creek
Brisbane
Queensland 4010
☎ (07) 26 28 955

897 High Street
Armadale
Melbourne
Vic 3143
☎ 50 90 360

21 Howard Street
Perth
WA 6000
☎ (09) 48 13 622

2 Kingsland Road
Bexley
Sydney, NSW 2207
☎ (02) 56 71 008

**Canada**
445 Wilbrod Street
Ottawa
Ontario KIN 6M7
☎ (613) 56 31 444

1131 Kensington Road NW
Calgary
Alta T2N 3P4
☎ (403) 28 36 526

Suite 710
1718 Argyle Street
Halifax
Nova Scotia B3J 3N6
☎ (902) 429 8200

1350 ouest, rue Sherbrooke
Suite 1030
Montréal, Qué H3G 1J1
☎ (514) 84 58 661

**UK**
18 Belgrave Mews West
London SW1 X 8HU
☎ (071) 23 53 731

Austrian Institute
28 Rutland Gate
London SW7 1PQ
☎ (071) 58 48 653-4

5 Barlows Road
Edgbaston
Birmingham B15 2PN
☎ (021) 45 41 197

33-34 Charlotte Square
Edinburgh EH2 4HF
☎ (31) 22 51 516

**USA**
2343 Massachusetts Avenue
NW
Washington DC 20008
☎ (202) 48 34 474

10 North Parkway Square
4200 North Side Parkway
NW
Atlanta GA 30327
☎ (404) 26 49 858

211 Congress Street
Suite 400
Boston MA 02110
☎ (617) 42 60 330

107 Delaware Avenue
Statler Bldg
Suite 828
Buffalo NY 14202
☎ (716) 85 27 000

Wrigley Building
Suite 707
400 North Michigan Avenue
Chicago, Illinois 60611
☎ (312) 22 21 515

1480 The Illuminating Building
55 Public Square
Cleveland, Ohio 44113
☎ (216) 62 15 588

First Interstate Tower South
Suite 2300
621 17th Street
Denver, Co 80293
☎ (303) 292 90 00

300 East Long Lake Road
Suite 375
Bloomfield Hills
Mi 48304
☎ (313) 64 51 444

5388 Poola Street
Honolulu
Hawaii 96821
☎ (808) 92 38 585 or 37 31 234

1535 West Loop South
Suite 319a
Houston
Texas 77029-9509
☎ (713) 62 32 233

4505 Madison Street
Kansas City
MO 64 111
☎ (816) 93 18 812

11859 Wilshire Boulevard
Suite 501
Los Angeles
California 90025
☎ (213) 44 49 310 or 47 34 721

Suite 200
Republic Building
1454 NW 17th Avenue
Miami, Florida 33125
☎(305)32 51 561

755 Magazine Street
New Orleans, LA 70130

31 East 69th Street
New York, N.Y. 10021
☎ (212) 73 76 400

Austrian Institute
Austrian Consulate General
Cultural Affairs Section
11 East 52nd Street
New York N.Y. 10022
☎ (212) 75 95 165

3 Parkway
20th Floor
Philadelphia, Pa 19102
☎ (215) 665 73 48

Austrian Consulate
c/o Bosrock & Company, Inc.
2490 World Trade Center
30 East 7th Street
Saint Paul, Minnesota 55101
☎ (612) 22 72 052

456 Montgomery Street
1000 San Francisco, CA 94104

c/o Hotel El San Juan and
Casino
Isla Verde
PR 00913
☎ (809) 791 2521

11th NE Penthouse 1
Seattle
Washington 98105
☎ (206) 63 33 606

Oxford Building
Suite 3a
141 North Meramec
Clayton, Missouri 63105
☎ (314) 96 67 687

## Facilities for Children

Many larger resorts have kindergartens for visitors' children. Many organise special activities such as parties, picnics, rambles, competitions, games, swimming, barbecues, sports, farm visits, etc. A number of villages have a baby-sitting service, and many hotels can supervise children throughout the day. Basic details may be obtained from the Austrian National Tourist Office while details of dates and times are obtainable from local tourist offices.

## Facilities for the Disabled

Austrian Federal Railways (OBB) have lightweight portable wheelchairs which are used for lifting people onto trains, and which can then be manoeuvred within the train. The chairs must be booked at least 3 days in advance and are bookable at any railway station in Austria at no extra cost. Advance bookings for journeys on Austrian Federal Railways can be made through local British Rail Travel Centres or rail-appointed travel agents.

The national organisation representing disabled people may be able to give general advice to travellers. Contact:
Allgemeine Unfallversicherungsanstalt
Adalbert Stifter-Strasse 65, A-1200 Vienna

## Festivals

Ask for local calendar events at the tourist information centres. Some of the major festivals are mentioned in this book.

## Health Regulations

In case of emergency or accident requiring a stay in hospital, the actual stay is free of charge though full payment has to be made for treatment and medication received. General practitioners' fees must also be paid in full. It is therefore advisable to take out private insurance. No vaccinations or inoculations are required by British visitors to Austria.

## Health Resorts

Austria has a number of health resorts and spas providing treatment for nearly all the diseases and complaints which respond to balneological or climatic therapy. All these are legally recognised and periodically subjected to scientific checks.

More details and lists of Austrian spas and health resorts can be obtained from the Austrian National Tourist Office and Österreichischer Heilbäder- und Kurorteverband
Josefsplatz 6, A-1010 Vienna
☎ 1/512 19 04

# Maps

Maps can be obtained from bookshops and local tourist information centres in Austria. *Kompass Wanderkarte* and *Mayr Wanderkarte* produce a series of walking maps which can be obtained locally. The *Mayr Wanderkarte* series has literature in English, French and German. *Freytag and Bernt* maps are also recommended.

# Measurements

The metric system is used in Austria
1 kilogram (1,000 grams) = 2.2lb
1 litre = $1^3/_4$ pints
4.5 litres = 1 gallon
1 kilometre = 0.62 miles (10km = approximately 6 miles).

# Post Offices

Post Offices are generally open Monday to Friday from 8am-12noon and from 2-6pm. Main and station post offices in larger cities are open round the clock, including Saturdays, Sundays and public holidays. Monetary transactions in all post offices, Monday to Friday up to 5pm.

Postage stamps are available not only in post offices but also in tobacco kiosks. Letter boxes are painted yellow or orange.

# Public Holidays

New Year's Day (1 January)
Epiphany (6 January)
Easter Monday
Labour Day (1 May)

Ascension Day
Whit Monday
Corpus Christi Day
Assumption of the Virgin (15 August)
National Holiday (26 October)
All Saint's Day (1 November)
Feast of the Immaculate Conception (8 December)
Christmas Day and Boxing Day (25 and 26 December)

## *Restaurants*

Lunch is served between 12noon and 2pm, dinner is available from 6pm onwards. A service charge of 10-15 per cent is included in all bills in restaurants, hotels etc. When satisfied with the service it is customary to give a tip amounting to around 5 per cent of the bill.

The cost of meals is lower than in the UK and this also applies to beer and wine by the glass. Hard drinks, tea and coffee tend to be more expensive.

**Menu**

Typical menu items are

*Leberknödelsuppe* — One of the many kinds of beef broth with added attractions (in this case liver dumplings)

*Schwammerlsuppe* — A rich soup of wild mushrooms seasoned with marjoram

*Kartoffelsuppe* — Thick potato soup made with sour cream and caraway

*Geräuchertes Forellenfilet* — Smoked fillet of trout, served with whipped cream and horseradish

*Gebackene Champignons* — Button mushrooms fried in breadcrumbs and served with sauce tartare

*Cordon Bleu* — A folded escalope of veal filled with ham and cheese and fried in breadcrumbs

*Zwiebelrostbraten* — Cut of roast beef served with a rich gravy and rings of onion

*Tafelspitz* — A delicate cut of boiled beef served with chives sauce and apple puree with horseradish

*Wildschweinbraten* — Roast wild boar in tender slices, with bread dumplings and cranberries

*Rehfilet* — Fillet of venison, again with dumplings and cranberries

*Bauernschmaus* — A rustic banquet all on one plate: roast pork and boiled ham, sauerkraut and a dumpling

*Palatschinken* — Pancakes, with a variety of fillings: curds and raisins, jam, chopped nuts and chocolate sauce (whipped cream optional)

*Marillenknödel* — Sweet dumplings with apricots inside and breadcrumbs and melted butter outside

*Salzburger Nockerin* — A riotous soufflé delicately flavoured with lemon

# *Shopping*

Most shops are open from Monday to Friday from 8am to 6.30pm with a one- or two-hour break at midday (there is no uniform system), and Saturday up to 1pm though this may vary from place to place. Smokers' requisites are sold at tobacconists' (Tabak-Trafik) and in automatic vending machines (at the normal price). Cigarettes, cigars and tobacco are also on sale in hotels, restaurants, cafés and inns (for an extra charge).

In shops displaying a 'Tax Free' sticker foreign visitors can apply for a refund of 24 per cent, 17 per cent or 9 per cent of the VAT on purchases in excess of AS 1,000. They should complete a customs declaration (form U-34). There is a small handling fee. When they leave the country they must present this form together with the purchases concerned to the customs authorities. Visitors leaving the country by train are advised to send their purchases as registered luggage. The baggage office clerk at the railway station will stamp and sign the customs declaration.

# *Sports and Pastimes*

### Canoeing
Canoeing is possible on a number of rivers in the Tyrol.
Further information from Tyrolean Water Sports Association:
(Tiroler Wasser Sportverein)
Franz-Fisher Strasse 23, Innsbruck A6020

### Cycle Hire
Cycle hire is available in many places, often including mountain bikes. There are some long cycle routes in Vorarlberg, including around Lake Constance; Bludenz to Walgau etc and many roads

have cycle lanes. Cycles may be hired at:

Axams                   Feldkirch
Bludenz                 Kossen
Bregenz                 Langenfeld
Burs                    Lienz
Ebbs                    Zell am Ziller

### Fishing
Fishing is possible at many resorts. Details from Austrian National Tourist Office, or local tourist offices.

### Golf
Golf courses are at:
Innsbruck
18 hole and 9 hole. Reached by car via Igls.
☎ (05223) 8177

Kitzbühel
9 hole
☎ (05356) 3070

Pertisau
9 hole
☎ (05243) 5377

Seefeld in Tyrol
18 hole
☎ (05212) 3003

St Johann in Tyrol
18 hole and 9 hole

The tourist information centres can provide detailed information.

### Mountaineering Schools, Mountain and Skiing Guides
Many towns and villages have climbing schools and local mountain guides. The ones recommended by the local tourist office will be of the high standard required by local regulations. The local tourist office will also be pleased to supply special brochures regarding mountaineering schools, mountain refuges, and alpine inns. These include suggestions for rambles and a list of Tyrolean mountain and skiing guides.

### Sailing
*Achenkirch*
Sailing School Achensee
A6215

*Bregenz*
Via the tourist office
15 Insel Strasse
☎ 05574 23391

*Buchau bei Maurach am Achensee*
Sailing Club Achensee
A6212

*Gerlos*
Sailing School Durlassboden Reservoir
A6281

*Reutte*
Sailing Club Plansee
A6600

Further information may be obtained from local tourist offices or
Tyrolean Water Sports Association (Tiroler Wasser Sportverein)
Franz-Fisher Strasse 23, A6020, Innsbruck.

## Skiing
Skiing is available at the high levels all year round on the glacier
areas such as Kaumertal, Stubai, Pitztal etc. Tourist offices have
lists of facilities in ski resorts. If you wish to obtain leaflets on a
certain region send an envelope with an international reply
coupon to the relevant Verkehrsamt.

*Highway Code for Skiers*
1. Be considerate towards other skiers.
2. Always ski within your own limits and gauge your speed to
   your own proficiency, to the terrain and to the prevailing
   weather conditions.
3. Pick your route in such a way as to avoid endangering others.
4. When overtaking another skier, leave enough room.
5. Before skiing into a downhill run or crossing a run, look uphill
   to ensure that you can do so without endangering yourself or
   others.
6. Do not stand around unnecessarily in blind corners or narrow
   sections of the run. If you fall, get out of the way as fast as
   possible.
7. Go uphill on skis or downhill on foot only in good visibility
   and at the edge of the marked piste.
8. It is essential that you comply with the slope markings and the
   instructions and warnings on notices. Anybody who disre-
   gards an avalanche warning or a 'Piste Closed' sign is risking
   their life.
9. Providing assistance in the case of an accident is mandatory.
10. Both those involved in an accident and eye-witnesses are
    required to give accurate personal particulars.

## Swimming
Almost every village has either an indoor or outdoor pool. Many
hotels allow visitors to use their pools.
   The following natural lakes have swimming facilities. Many

having changing cubicles, sun lawn, recreational areas, boat hire, fishing, restaurants, etc. The water temperature can reach 24 to 27°C (75 to 80°F) in summer.

*Achensee*
Largest and most beautiful of Tyrol's lakes. Bathing facilities at Pertisau, Maurach, Achenkirch, Gaisalm, and Seespitz

*Bodensee* (Lake Constance)

*Frauensee*
Near Lechaschau

*Piburgersee*
Near Oetz. One of the warmest lakes, amid dense woods

*Plansee*
Near Reutte. Surrounded by imposing mountains and lovely woods

*Reithersee*
In the centre of Reith in the Alpbach valley

*Schwarzsee*
Near Kitzbuhel. Warmest peat-water lake in the Tyrol (up to 27°C/81°F)

*Seefelder Wildsee*
Surrounded by the magnificent scenery of the Wetterstein, Mieminger and Karwendel ranges

*Stimmersee and Hechtsee*
Near Kufstein

*Thiersee*
North of Kufstein. Surrounded by meadows and mountains

*Tristachersee*
(East Tyrol)
In dense woods at foot of Lienzer Dolomites, south of Lienz

*Urisee*
East of Reutte. Surrounded by woods

*Walchsee*
North of the Kaiser Mountains

**Wind Surfing Schools**

*Achenkirch*
Sailing and Surfing School Achensee
Freidrich Schwaiger
Seeblick Inn
A6215

*Gerlos*
Surfing School Durlassboden Reservoir
Tourist Office Gerlos
A6281

*Haldensee*
Surfing School Groen-Haldensee
Sportsclub Montanara
Sport Hotel
A6673

*Kitzbühel*
Surfing School Pillersee
Heinz Mueller
Pfarrau 19a
A6370

*Kossen*
Surfing School Walchsee-
  Kossen
Sport Merkl
Department Store Payr
A6345

*Pertisau*
Surfing School Achensee
Dora Storm
St Hubertus Inn
A6213

*Reutte*
Surfing School Plansee
Arnold Winklmair
Hotel Forelle
A6600

Windsurfing is allowed on the following lakes:

*Achensee*
Permits from tourist offices in
Pertisau and Achenkirch
*Plansee*
Permits from Hotel Seespitze
and Hotel Forelle in Reutte
*Heiterwangersee*
*Haldensee*

*Durlassboden Reservoir*
*Hintersteinersee*
*Thiersee*
Permits from the bathing place
*Walchsee*
Permits from the Surfing School
(see the Kossen address above)

On Schwarzsee, near Kitzbuhel, and Tristachersee, near Tristach
in East Tyrol, windsurfing is limited to after 5pm and only if
swimmers are not disturbed. Permits from Schwarzsee bathing
place and Hotel Tristachersee.

## Taxis

In the larger cities taxis are provided with officially controlled
meters. In the case of fare changes, a supplement is added to the
charge shown. An extra charge is made for luggage. In smaller
towns, fixed charges for certain destinations apply, while the fare
for overland journeys is agreed upon beforehand.

## Telephones

To telephone abroad from Austria from a payphone first lift the
receiver; then insert coins (the slots take 1, 5, 10, 20 schilling coins).
When the dialling tone is audible dial 00 44 (for the UK) or 01 (for
USA and Canada) then the home number, including the area code

(but omit the initial 0 for the UK). Where there are only three coin slots press the red button when the dialled number answers. An audible tone warns that the time is about to expire. In hotels press the button on the handset then dial the number as before. Long distance telephone calls normally work out cheaper when made from a post office or public callbox, since hotels are entitled to levy surcharges.

Telephone numbers consist of a three, four, or six-figure number plus a four-figure prefix which is the area code. For calls made within Austria add the prefix 0; for calls from abroad add the relevant dialling code code for Austria, ie from the UK add 01043. Every Austrian telephone is connected to the direct dialling system. Trunk calls can also be put through by direct dialling to all European countries. Trunk calls within Austria and to 40 countries abroad including the United Kingdom and Ireland are approximately 35 per cent cheaper between 6pm and 8am as well on weekends (from Friday 6pm to Monday 8am) and public holidays.

**Useful Telephone Numbers**
ÖAMTC emergency breakdown service: 120
ARBÖ emergency breakdown service: 123
Fire brigade: 122
Police: 133
Ambulance: 144 (no area codes are necessary)

## *Tourist Offices*

The main Austrian National Tourist Offices are:

**UK**
Austrian National Tourist
    Office
30 St George Street
London W1R 0AL
☎ (071) 629 0461

**Austria**
Urlaubsinformation Österreich
Margaretenstrasse 1
A-1040 Wien
☎ (1) 58 72 000

**Canada**
Austrian National Tourist
    Office
736 Granville Street
Vancouver Block
Suite 1220
Vancouver, BC V6Z 1J2
☎ 604 683 5808

Austrian National Tourist
   Office
2 Bloor Street East, Suite 3330
Toronto
Ontario M4W 1A8
☎ 416 967 3380

Austrian National Tourist
   Office
1010 Sherbrooke Street West
Suite 1410
Montreal PQ H3A 2R7
☎ 514 849 3709

**USA**
Austrian National Tourist
   Office
500 Fifth Avenue
Suite 2009-2022
New York, NY 10110
☎ (212) 944 6880

Austrian National Tourist
   Office
11601 Wilshire Blvd, Suite 2480
Los Angeles
California 90025
☎ (213) 477-3332

**Tyrol**
Tirol Werbung
Bozner Platz 6
A-6010 Innsbruck
☎ (512) 53 20/170

**Vorarlberg**
Vorarlberg-Tourismus
Römerstrasse 7/I
A-6901 Bregenz
☎ (5574) 42 5 25-0

Detailed information may be obtained from the *Verkehrsvereine/Verkehrsamt* (local tourist offices) or *Kurkommissionen* (spa administrations) of the individual resorts and from the provincial tourist boards. Tourist offices in Austria are usually open from 8am-12noon with 2 hours for lunch and from 2-5 or 6pm depending on the season. They are usually open until later in the summer. Most villages also have an information point. In some cases literature is available 24 hours a day, and includes details of available accommodation, walks in the area, skiing facilities etc. Visitors cards offer special reductions on leisure activities in certain regions. You may be eligible for a Guest Card which also acts as a discount card. Ask for details. Some of the tourist offices act as booking agencies for accommodation in the area.

If writing, letters sent to the Verkehrsverein at the town concerned with the postal code given in the Additional Information is a sufficient address.

# *Travel*

Austria is very easy to reach. One may take the car ferry to Vlissingen, Ostend or Zeebrugge from Britain, then the Belgian and German motorways by way of Cologne. Another route is through northern France via Strasbourg and Lake Constance. The fastest way is via the German motorways and, for the time-conscious traveller, it is possible to drive from the Belgian ports almost to the Austrian border without leaving the motorway.

## By Air

Air connections to Austria are provided by Austrian Airlines, Lauda Air, Tyrolean Airways and many foreign air companies. International airlines call at the following airports: Vienna, Graz, Innsbruck, Klagenfurt, Linz and Salzburg.

## By Rail

The Austrian Federal Railways have a total length of about 5,800 rail-kilometres (3,600 miles). There are rapid and frequent direct connections with all European countries. Seat reservations are possible. The Austrian Federal Railways have introduced an hourly or two-hourly intercity service connecting Vienna with Salzburg, Graz, Innsbruck and Villach. Various fare reductions are granted, such as: cross-country rail pass, rail passes for the individual provinces, Rabbit Card and Rabbit Card Junior (valid on 4 days at choice within 10 day period), Eurail Pass, Inter-Rail Pass, discounts for senior citizens and groups as well as reduced return tickets for distances up to 70km (43 miles). Children up to 6 years of age travel free of charge as long as no seat is claimed for them. Children aged 6 to 15 inclusive pay only 50 per cent of the full (or reduced) fare. Passengers travelling over 71km (40 miles) may interrupt the journey but must have their tickets stamped accordingly by the ticket inspector.

Express trains have dining cars, during the night trains have sleeping cars and couchettes. It is advisable to obtain route and schedule information in advance as these vary according to season. Railway ticket offices, travel agencies, automobile clubs and the Central Railway Information in Vienna, ☎ (1) 17 17 will provide precise information and rates.

Vehicles and trailers may be transported by rail through the Tauern Tunnel (Böckstein-Mallnitz, 8km (5 miles); transport in either direction according to the appropriate summer or winter train schedule. Information at the railway stations of Böckstein, ☎ (64 34) 26 63-39, and Mallnitz, ☎ (47 84) 230-33.

## By Road
In the Alps gradients from one in seventeen to steeper than one in seven may be encountered. The edges of nearly all mountain roads are fitted with guard-rails. On steep downhill gradients it is important to engage a low gear in due time. On narrow mountain roads there is no binding priority rule; the vehicle which can more easily reverse to a passing place is obliged to do so. On snowy surfaces winter tyres, studded tyres (permissible from 15 November to the first Sunday after Easter) and in extreme cases snow chains are essential. The two Austrian Automobile Clubs (ÖAMTC and ARBÖ) have rental facilities for snow chains.

*Automobile Clubs*
ARBÖ (Auto-, Motor- und Radfahrerbund Österreichs)
Mariahilfer Strasse 80, A-1150 Vienna
☎ (222) 85 35 35

ÖAMTC (Österreichischer Automobil-, Motorrad und Touring-club)
Schubertring 1-3, A-1010 Vienna
☎ (222) 711 99-0

## Coach
Bus and motor coach services in Austria are run by federal and local authorities as well as by private companies. Altogether about 1,800 scheduled lines are in operation. Some 70 international coach services (including 1 Europabus service) travel to or through Austria. Motor coach excursions are organised by local bus companies from all tourist resorts to the surroundings as well as to more distant goals, and partly also to foreign countries.

## By Sea
*Car Ferry Routes*
Dover or Folkestone to Ostend or Dunkirk by Sealink.
Dover or Felixtowe to Zeebrugge by P&O Ferries.
Sheerness to Vlissingen by Olau Lines.
All quickly join the continental motorway system.
Harwich to the Hook of Holland is another Sealink service.

British tourists need only a valid driving licence and the car log book, though you are still advised to obtain a 'Green Card' international insurance card from your own insurance company before leaving home.

**Driving Regulations**
A valid UK licence is acceptable in Austria, and although language difficulties may give rise to misunderstanding in a few isolated cases, it is legally valid. The minimum age at which a visitor may use a temporarily imported car or motorcycle (exceeding 50cc) is 18 years. The Austrian motoring club (ÖAMTC) will supply a free translation of your licence into German, but this is only available from their head office in Vienna.

Children under the age of 12 are not allowed to sit next to the driver: they must be on the back seat. The wearing of seatbelts is obligatory.

In Austria drive on the right-hand side of the road. Maximum speed on trunk roads is 100kmh (62mph) and on motorways 130km (81mph). In built up areas (between the place name signs) the limit is 50kmh (31mph) if not otherwise stated. For cars with trailers exceeding $^3/_4$ tons: outside built up areas 80kmh (50mph) on motorways 100km (62mph). Additional speed limits can be imposed when necessary.

Drunken driving is punishable by a fine and confiscation of a driving licence. Permissible alcohol limit: blood 0.8%; breath 0.4%.

Limited parking zones (blue zones) with a maximum parking time of 3 hours are clearly marked as such. Parking clocks can be obtained free of charge in tobacconists' shops (Tabak-Trafik). In a few towns there is a charge for parking vouchers, which can be obtained in banks, some petrol stations and most tobacconists'; they must be clearly displayed on the inside of the windscreen.

Drivers are required to report immediately to the police all traffic accidents involving injury to persons. Accidents involving material damage must only be reported when mutual identity has not been established. Please use the accident registration form provided by the Comité Européen des Assurances. On motorways and main roads the Austrian automobile clubs operate an emergency breakdown service which may be utilised by anyone.

In Austria, all vehicles (including motorcycles) must be equipped with a first-aid kit by law, and visitors are expected to comply.

This item will not be checked at the frontier, but motorists can be stopped at the scene of an accident and their first-aid kit demanded; if this is not forthcoming the police may take action.

It is compulsory for motorcyclists (rider and passenger) to wear crash helmets.

Austrian traffic regulations are similar to those in force in other European countries. For driving in Austria during the winter months, winter tyres are essential and in extreme cases, snow chains have to be used. These can be hired at all major border crossings.

### Useful Road Signs

*Ausfahrt* — Exit from motorway or dual carriageway
*Bankett nicht befahrbar* — Soft verges
*Einbahnstrasse* — One-way street
*Einordnen* — Get in lane
*Freie Fahrt* — End of restrictions, usually after passing roadworks
*Gegenverkehr* — Oncoming traffic
*Glatteisgefahr* — Danger on icy road
*Langsam fahren* — Drive slowly
*Rollsplit* — Loose chippings
*Umleitung* (on yellow arrow) — Traffic diversion
*Links/Rechts fahren* — Drive on the left/right

### Car Hire

All the major international car-hire firms have offices in Austria. Facilities are available at international airports, in larger cities, and at the railway stations of Bregenz, Dornbirn, Innsbruck, and Jenbach.

### Fuel

*Credit cards* In general filling stations do not accept credit cards.
*Duty-free fuel* In addition to the fuel in the vehicle tank, up to 10 litres in a can may be imported free of customs duty and tax.
*Fuel (leaded)* Super benzin (98 octane) grade available.
*Fuel (unleaded)* is sold in Austria as Normal benzin (91 octane) and Eurosuper benzin (9 octane) grades. Pumps dispensing unleaded fuel are marked with a green point or label indicating *Euro 95* or *Eurosuper* or *bleifrei*. The octane rating is clearly marked on the individual pumps, except for those in a few non-brand garages. The *Selbst Dienst* sign means Self Service.

### Traffic News

Hourly after the news bulletin on the hour, on the station Ö3. Reports of serious holdups (traffic jams, accidents, weather-related traffic problems) are broadcast in the affected area as they are received and repeated after the hourly news bulletins on Ö3.

Blue Danube Radio broadcasts traffic news in English between 7 and 9am, 12noon and 2pm and in case of serious holdups between 6 and 7.30pm (on the FM waveband: Vienna 103.8 and 92.4 MHz, Styria 101.4 MHz, Carinthia 102.3 MHz, Tyrol 101.4 and 102.3 MHz, Upper Austria 92.6 and 102.0 MHz).

### Toll Roads In The Tyrol

TYROL/ITALY

**Brenner Motorway**

From Innsbruck (Austria) to Bolzano (Italy). Only cars, minibuses and motorbikes are permitted on the Italian section of the road. Coaches, cars with luggage or caravan trailers and heavy vehicles are prohibited.

**Timmelsjoch Alpine Road**

Open: May to October

TYROL/VORARLBERG

**Arlberg Road Tunnel**

Silvretta Alpine Road

Open: June to mid-October. No cars with caravans or heavy vehicles.

TYROL/SALZBURG

**Gerlosplatte-Krimml**

Open: all year

Toll-free on the Tyrolean side, toll payable on Salzburg side.

EAST TYROL/SALZBURG

**Felbertauern Road**

TYROL

**Absam-Eichat-Halltal**

Closed in winter. No coaches.

**Aschau** (see Zillertal road)

**Ellmay-Wochenbrunner Alm**
Open: all year. Only cars and minibuses.
Toll refundable as refreshments at Gasthof Wochenbrunn.

**Ginzling TWK** (Tyrolean power works)
Open: May to October
Private road to the Schlegeis reservoir.

**Gnadenwald-Hinterhornalm**
Open: May to November.

**Grinzens-Keinater Alm**
Open: summer only
Cars and minibuses only.

**Hinterniss-Eng**
Open: May to November
Reached from Germany.

**Hippach** (see Zillertal road)

**Kaltenbach** (see Zillertal road)

**Kaunertal**
Open: May to December
Prinz-Weisseeferner, from Gepatsch reservoir toll payable.
Holders of ski pass free of charge.

**Kirchdorf-Kaiserbachtal-Griesener Alm**
Open: Easter to early November

**Kitzbüheler Horn Mountain Road**
Open: May to October
Toll refundable as refreshments at Alpengasthof.

**Landl** (see Thiersee-Landl-Achernalm)

**Matrei am Brenner-Maria Waldrast**

**Maurach-Achenkirch**
Open: June to October
Old Achensee road.

**Mayrhofen-Gasthof Wasserfall**
Open: May to October

**Pertisau-Falzthurnalm-Gramaialm**
(or Pertisau-Pletzachalm-Gernalm)
Open: May to October.

**Ried/Zillertal** (see Zillertal road)

**Solden-Rettenbachferner-Tiefenbachferner**
Open: May to December
Ötztal glaciers road.

**Thiersee-Landl-Achernalm**
Open: summer only
Cars and minibuses only.

**Waidring-Steinplatte Mountain Road**

**Weer-Nafingersee-Weidener Huette**
(or Weer-Saga Alm)

**Zell am Ziller** (see Zillertal road)

**Zillertal Mountain Road**
(Hippach-Zellberg-Aschau-Kaltenbach-Ried)
Open: mid-June to end September.

EAST TYROL
**Iselberg-Zwischenbergen**
Open: summer only

**Iselberg-Roaner Alm**
Open: June to mid-October

**Kals-Glockner Road**
(Kals-Koednitztal)
Toll-free in winter.

**Lienz-Thurn-Zettersfeld**
Matrei in Osttirol-Matreier Tauernhaus-Innergschloss
Up to 9am and from 5pm use limited. Only passable in summer.
Only single-track vehicles, cars and minibuses.

**St Jacob in Defereggen-Erisbach-Oberhausalm**
Open: June to September only
Only single-track vehicles and cars.

**Thal-Assling-Hochstein Road**
(Bannberg Café-Bannberger Alpe)
Open: all year

**Tristach-Kreithof-Dolomitenhuette**
Open: mid-May to early October

> **Distances between the main towns and cities in Austria in kilometres**
> **(1 mile = 1.6km)**

| From \ To | Zell am See | Vienna | Villach | Spittal an der Drau | St Pölten | St Johann in Tyrol | Salzburg | Reutte | Mariazell | Linz | Liezen | Landeck | Kufstein | Krems | Klagenfurt | Bad Ischl | Innsbruck | Horn | Graz | Feldkirch | Eisenstadt | Brenner | Bregenz | Bischofshofen |
|---|---|---|---|---|---|---|---|---|---|---|---|---|---|---|---|---|---|---|---|---|---|---|---|---|
| **Vienna** | 386 | | | | | | | | | | | | | | | | | | | | | | | |
| **Villach** | 353 | 397 | | | | | | | | | | | | | | | | | | | | | | |
| **Spittal an der Drau** | 186 | 331 | 37 | | | | | | | | | | | | | | | | | | | | | |
| **St Pölten** | 322 | 68 | 331 | 326 | | | | | | | | | | | | | | | | | | | | |
| **St Johann in Tyrol** | 65 | 370 | 215 | 176 | 310 | | | | | | | | | | | | | | | | | | | |
| **Salzburg** | 82 | 300 | 183 | 146 | 240 | 72 | | | | | | | | | | | | | | | | | | |
| **Reutte** | 270 | 543 | 392 | 348 | 483 | 185 | 245 | | | | | | | | | | | | | | | | | |
| **Mariazell** | 297 | 137 | 258 | 253 | 77 | 379 | 307 | 529 | | | | | | | | | | | | | | | | |
| **Linz** | 217 | 186 | 315 | 275 | 126 | 204 | 132 | 377 | 148 | | | | | | | | | | | | | | | |
| **Liezen** | 143 | 248 | 225 | 154 | 227 | 206 | 126 | 374 | 155 | 121 | | | | | | | | | | | | | | |
| **Landeck** | 97 | 476 | 114 | 71 | 445 | 105 | 191 | 277 | 331 | 340 | 225 | | | | | | | | | | | | | |
| **Kufstein** | 247 | 523 | 373 | 329 | 464 | 166 | 226 | 71 | 486 | 191 | 355 | 258 | | | | | | | | | | | | |
| **Krems** | 105 | 400 | 252 | 213 | 333 | 33 | 96 | 165 | 370 | 277 | 235 | 136 | 149 | | | | | | | | | | | |
| **Klagenfurt** | 358 | 80 | 367 | 362 | 30 | 346 | 276 | 519 | 113 | 206 | 162 | 432 | 500 | 377 | | | | | | | | | | |
| **Bad Ischl** | 221 | 325 | 37 | 69 | 294 | 256 | 220 | 428 | 247 | 318 | 263 | 409 | 293 | 330 | | | | | | | | | | |
| **Innsbruck** | 125 | 268 | 235 | 195 | 208 | 129 | 57 | 302 | 230 | 102 | 151 | 244 | 206 | 409 | 270 | | | | | | | | | |
| **Horn** | 178 | 451 | 300 | 256 | 391 | 93 | 153 | 92 | 413 | 285 | 202 | 185 | 282 | 160 | 69 | 283 | 244 | 210 | | | | | | |
| **Graz** | 398 | 86 | 402 | 407 | 70 | 386 | 316 | 559 | 153 | 303 | 472 | 540 | 222 | 540 | 185 | 336 | 284 | 467 | 401 | 266 | | | | |
| **Feldkirch** | 260 | 198 | 172 | 203 | 186 | 256 | 326 | 493 | 113 | 231 | 119 | 222 | 40 | 286 | 135 | 183 | 367 | 157 | 624 | 558 | | | | |
| **Eisenstadt** | 302 | 457 | 413 | 548 | 70 | 310 | 256 | 570 | 442 | 439 | 84 | 233 | 579 | 130 | 494 | 300 | 157 | 624 | 558 | 558 | | | | |
| **Brenner** | 363 | 50 | 337 | 323 | 110 | 432 | 343 | 600 | 139 | 225 | 580 | 444 | 108 | 372 | 243 | 294 | 131 | 173 | 651 | | | | | |
| **Bregenz** | 212 | 486 | 336 | 289 | 424 | 126 | 186 | 126 | 446 | 318 | 315 | 108 | 455 | 189 | 501 | 434 | 190 | 527 | | | | | | |
| **Bischofshofen** | 334 | 357 | 135 | 136 | 300 | 51 | 283 | 322 | 190 | 94 | 135 | 261 | 139 | 332 | 171 | 112 | 188 | 366 | 212 | 345 | 318 | 221 | 377 | |
| **Arlberg** | 47 | 254 | 409 | 365 | 500 | 37 | 294 | 391 | 394 | 262 | 107 | 522 | 185 | 536 | 319 | 445 | 109 | 556 | 510 | 616 | 142 | 90 | 298 | |

# INDEX

# MPC

## A Note to the Reader

Thank you for buying this book, we hope it has helped you to enjoy your visit to Tyrol and the Verarlberg. We have worked hard to produce a guidebook which is as accurate as possible. With this in mind, any comments, suggestions or useful information you may have would be appreciated.

Please send your letters to:
The Editor
Moorland Publishing Co Ltd
Moor Farm Road West
Ashbourne
Derbyshire
DE6 1HD

*The Travel Specialists*